D0465547

Intimate Spaces

*A Conversation about
Discovery and Connection*

To all the *humans being* in my life. Thank you for co-creating spaces with me where good things have happened.

To everyone searching and hoping for *intimate spaces.*

The truth is that the highest praise one can bestow upon a scientist is not to say of him that he is a fact-grubber but that he is a man of imagination. It was John Dewey who observed that every great advance in science has issued from a new audacity of the imagination.

—Ashley Montagu, *Growing Young*, p. 132

All actual life is encounter.

—Martin Buber, I and Thou, p. 62.

Intimate Spaces

*A Conversation about
Discovery and Connection*

Douglas L. Kelley

Arizona State University

cognella®
SAN DIEGO

Bassim Hamadeh, CEO and Publisher
Todd R. Armstrong, Publisher
Tony Paese, Project Editor
Christian Berk, Production Editor
Jess Estrella, Senior Graphic Designer
Stephanie Kohl, Licensing Associate
Natalie Piccotti, Director of Marketing
Kassie Graves, Vice President of Editorial
Jamie Giganti, Director of Academic Publishing

Cover image copyright © 2018 iStockphoto LP/grynold.
copyright © 2018 iStockphoto LP/smartboy10.
copyright © 2015 iStockphoto LP/smartboy10.

Printed in the United States of America.

3970 Sorrento Valley Blvd., Ste. 500, San Diego, CA 92121

CONTENTS

CONVERSATION THREE
Experiencing Intimacy: Connecting and Becoming

ACKNOWLEDGMENTS

am grateful to numerous persons for their participation in this endeavor. To begin, I am thankful to my students in countless ways. Over the past twenty years I have been testing ideas with them and they have been engaging me with thoughtful challenge and response. Some of these ideas came through assignments specifically designed for me to hear from my students. I added these assignments to my courses after my sabbatical in 2016. Interestingly, the most common question I received after my sabbatical was, "Did you have a productive sabbatical?" Well, you'll have to tell me. Much of my sabbatical was given to re-approaching my teaching, hearing more from my students, and rethinking my writing. So thank you to ASU for providing support for this project and my teaching. And to an absolutely incredible Human Subjects department who provided support for this research.

Another arm of ASU that has been wonderfully encouraging is the Lincoln Center for Applied Ethics. As Professor of Relationship Ethics, I have been supported in various ways by the Lincoln Center, including financial help to pay some of the graduate students who worked on this project. Thank you, Jason, for being out of the box.

I owe a huge debt to undergraduate and graduate students who served on my research team. Special thanks to Mary Zatezalo who was project manager for data collection and analysis of the *Intimacy in Personal Relationships* study. Thank you, Mary, for taking charge of many of the research tasks and handling problems with creativity and grace. Thank you to Hannah Nichols and Darbie Hall, both of whom began this project as undergraduates through an NCUIRE grant from ASU, and morphed into our graduate program still working for me. I appreciate all of your energy and insights, but especially all of the times we all had together working the data and new ideas. Special thanks to Hannah, who consolidated the final details of the analysis—I appreciate your good eye for detail and unquenchable enthusiasm. Also, thanks to Kerstin Gallardo, a graduate student who did much of the preliminary research for *Conversations One* and *Two* and quite a bit of early editing. My letter of recommendation is waiting for you when you are ready to pursue your Ph.D.

Also, thank you to the Cognella staff, in particular Todd Armstrong who has believed in and supported my work for many years, and Tony Pease and Christian Berk who have picked up many of the details as we have moved toward publication. Thanks, especially, for your patience when life threw me a curveball late in the process.

Recently Vince Waldron told me he recommended hiring me, 25 years ago, because of my early intimacy work. Vince, you've been a tremendous friend and colleague.

Finally, thank you to my wife, Ann. Quite plainly, the book is a better read because of your careful, insightful editing. And to those of you who have trouble with certain sections of the book, that's not Ann's fault—those are surely places where I chose not to take her advice. But, more than that, thanks Ann for hanging in there with me (or letting me hang with you). I have learned and grown so much over the past 43 years of our dating and marriage. Thank you for your openness, steadfastness, patience, and willingness to grow and forgive. Thank you for being a partner interested in creating *Intimate Spaces.*

INTIMATE SPACES

A CONVERSATION ABOUT
DISCOVERY AND CONNECTION

Thich Nhat Hanh, a Buddhist monk and teacher living in the south of France suggests that, "When you hold a child in your arms, or hug your mother, or your husband, or your friend, if you breathe in and out three times, your happiness will be multiplied at least tenfold."[1] I tried this simple exercise with my family and the results were quite remarkable. For me, at some point during breath number two I began to relax and truly be present with the other person. I've since suggested the exercise to numerous others and the responses are fascinating. Some people almost melt into your arms with no rush to break the embrace. Others are tight the entire time—they never actually let you into their personal space. Still others joke and laugh to keep this uncomfortable hug at a safe emotional distance.

Intimate spaces. Elusive. Alluring. Exhilarating. Frightening.

The challenge of intimacy is ever present. Most of us spend inordinate amounts of time pursuing it, even if we don't know that intimacy is really what we're after. Yet, like a butterfly fluttering in seemingly random patterns, intimacy often evades our grasp. When this elusive wonder unexpectedly does land on our relationship noses we may find ourselves startled by its presence, reacting with awkward excitement or shock or fear. At such times we run the risk of inadvertently sending this relational beauty on its way, crushing it as we cling with excitement, or running the other way as if this flighty creature carried the plague!

In an odd paradox of nature, intimacy—like the evasive butterfly—most often lights gently on us when we give up chasing it. In fact, it often shows up when we are busy about other things—in the midst of conflict, during the hug of forgiveness, while chatting on a long walk, or when playfully bantering with one's lover after sex. It is wonderfully freeing to realize that we can't

---

1 Thich Nhat Hanh, *Peace is Every Step* (New York: Bantam Books, 1991), 85.

make intimacy happen, we can only *create a space where if it can happen, it will*. Thus, the title of this book, *Intimate Spaces*.

The unpredictable nature of intimacy offers freedom as it eliminates the pressure to somehow do this relationship thing "right." But for most of us it simultaneously creates a sense of uncertainty and vulnerability as we give up the ability to control this essential aspect of our lives—"What if I reach out and she doesn't reciprocate?", "What if he leaves me?", "What if my closest friend moves and I'm left alone?", "Will my wayward son ever return home?", "What am I supposed to do, just sit and wait for the 'ideal' partner to drop by?". The raw openness of this process fills many of us with fear and leads us to retreat and take solace in solitude, or alternatively to create structure, control, and role-based relationships that offer a false sense of protection from being hurt.

That said, for most of us, the glimpses of intimacy we do experience, whether intentionally or simply because we happened to relationally show up one day, keep us coming back for more. Because intimacy is founded on authentic presence with another human being, it is an invigorating risk when it pays off. True intimacy is exhilarating. The startling beauty, vulnerability, and fragility engage all our senses. And true intimacy brings joy and healing as we experience being known and accepted by another human being.

Intimate Challenges

We are *made for intimacy*. From the endorphins flooding mother's and child's bodies during the birth process to the slow adolescent development toward independent adulthood, from the fascinating connection between affection and psychological and physical health to the sometimes irrational pursuit of certain friendships and romantic relationships as adults, the signs are clear—intimacy is an essential part of human experience.

This tug toward intimacy, however, is a relative mystery to many of us. We want it, but the path is filled with roadblocks—we often don't think about intimacy in constructive ways, we may have residual pain from intimate partners, and we are often simply bad at doing it (later I will challenge the idea that intimacy is something we do). My research and conversations with students and friends consistently reveal people's tendency to confuse sex with intimacy, view intimacy as only pertinent to romantic relationships, and experience intimacy as underwhelming at best and hurtful at worst.

In addition to these personal challenges, anemic portrayals of intimacy in the media have complicated matters. The other day on a morning news program I watched an interview with a woman who was billed as an "intimacy expert." The only thing the "expert" talked about during her interview was innovative ways to have sex. In fact, she suggested that you go to the local drug store and take a stroll down the "intimacy aisle" to find new ideas to spice up your sex life. In terms of spicing up your sex life this is not a bad idea, but ... the *intimacy* aisle? Her comment reinforces the ideas that intimacy is synonymous with sex or is something you can somehow purchase or obtain by learning the newest technique. The expert never mentioned anything about emotional connection between partners, or how roaming *together* down the "intimacy aisle" and being playful with one another may actually bring the intimacy you are hoping to find.

Another intimacy challenge is that there are few places to learn about a rich, full perspective on intimacy. Because intimacy is both communicative and psychological we must learn how to communicate care, affection, and love to our relational partners as well as create safe spaces where we give others deep access to our inner selves and allow them to do the same. One example of the scant opportunities to learn about intimacy is evident when I ask my students how many of them had the "sex talk" with their parents (or other family members). An extremely low number report they have had "the talk" (generally under 10% of the class, in spite of the fact that surveys of parents suggest otherwise[2]). When I ask those who said they had "the talk" with their parents to describe the content of the talk, they typically report that their parents made sure they knew the basic mechanics of sex. And, safe sex was generally discussed in terms of *not* getting pregnant and *not* getting diseases. Important topics for sure. But in *Intimate Spaces* we will talk about "safe sex" as the key to experiencing sexual intimacy through the creation of *safe emotional spaces* for one another to grow and become. And more than that, we will explore the opportunity for emotional connectedness in our close friendships and family relationships.

Intimate Conversations

Intimate Spaces is a conversation about discovery and connection. I am inviting you to talk about, muse, ponder, and experience intimacy. Even though I have written and taught about intimacy for years, *Intimate Spaces* is not an intimacy answer book. Instead, it is an honest conversation. I aim to engage you in a dialogue, of sorts. Recently, psychotherapist Ester Perel stated that

---

2 A. Carter, "Are Parents Having the Sex Talk with Their Kids?," HuffPost, November 1, 2017.

because of our rapidly changing times there are no relationship experts in today's world. Even though she is known internationally for her relationship expertise, she describes herself as a "learner."[3] In this same spirit, the ideas that emerge in the following pages largely come from listening and observing. They have been tossed back and forth with others, like playing catch on a summer's day. They have been mulled over, chewed upon, and wrestled with. In *Intimate Spaces*, I hope to engage you as a reader in this intimate conversation.

The discussions we will have throughout the following pages are designed to be intellectually challenging. Using a broad range of social science research, I will launch us into the murky, conceptual territory of intimacy. In a recent study I conducted, *Intimacy in Personal Relationships* (IPR), designed in part for this book, I asked people for their perspectives on intimacy and love, and to provide examples of how intimacy with others emerged through talk, play, grief, forgiveness, conflict and, of course, sex. Throughout the book, I provide examples from the stories and anecdotes participants generously shared. However, to keep the conversation alive, each section asks *you* to consider these same aspects of intimacy as together we explore these topics.

For this book to really work, our *Intimate Spaces* conversations must also embody intimacy itself. If I present interesting ideas and research findings, but fail to create an intimate space between us, this book will be lifeless words on a screen or page—some 'nice' or, even, good ideas, but, nevertheless, a book that will leave you and me unchanged. To this end, throughout the book I use *Growing Close* sections to ask for your thoughts and reflections. And, in case you're wondering, I'm not off the hook either. As the conversations unfold you will hear parts of my own story and struggle with intimacy, both at a personal and professional level.

Beginning the Conversation

I've designed *Intimate Spaces* around three conversations (parts), each of which is comprised of eight threads (chapters). Each thread varies in length, as they do in face-to-face conversations. The first conversation, *The Essence of Intimacy: Discovery and Connection,* is focused on exploring the very nature of

---

3 Esther Perel and Peter Sagal, "Not My Job: We Quiz Couples Therapist Esther Perel On The Monastic Life," June 10, 2017, in *Wait Wait ... Don't Tell Me!,* produced by Mike Danforth, podcast, https://www.npr.org/2017/06/10/532171202/not-my-job-we-quiz-couples-therapist-esther-perel-on-the-monastic-life.

intimacy. Here we unpack social science thinking on relational closeness, but also ask some messy questions, such as, Why is intimacy such a significant aspect of life? How do I think about my *self* in relationship to my partner's self? What do I do with the vulnerability that is inherent to intimate relationships? How is intimacy related to other relationship experiences, such as love and trust? And perhaps most importantly, how can I understand intimacy as an agent of transformation in my relationships and for our individual "selfs"?[4]

Embracing fresh understandings of intimacy requires us to dispel common perspectives that limit our personal and relational experiences. These perspectives guide the second conversation, *Myths that Inhibit Discovery, Connection, and Being*. For instance, it's commonly presumed that women are better at intimacy than men. And, while there may be some truth to this perspective, what I've learned from research, teaching, and my own personal experience is that we all struggle with "doing" intimacy. I know many women who have little idea what intimacy is and, regarding what they do know about intimacy, often settle for less in their relationships. And, perhaps surprising to some of you, I know many men who desperately desire intimacy but have no idea how to articulate what they are really looking for. Other common ideas that need to be reexamined are that sex equals intimacy, intimacy only occurs with your "soulmate," you can lose your identity in intimacy, and that intimacy is primarily something you "do."

The final conversation, *Experiencing Intimacy: Connecting and Becoming*, explores surprising spaces for intimacy to emerge, and some unexpected ways to *be intimate*. I begin this conversation with a discussion of what it means to experience an *intimate moment*. As we explore mindfulness, reciprocal sharing, and meaningfulness it will become clearer as to why intimacy-like moments may feel incomplete. However, each thread of this conversation will introduce new possibilities of creating intimate relationship spaces. There is a playfulness to many of the threads in this section because play is one of the ways we can become intimate with one another. Yet we will also explore the flip side. For example, grief offers fertile ground for intimacy to grow, as does the vulnerability of open conflict and forgiveness. Of course, sex can be an intimate act, but learning to make sex an act of connection, a way of being and discovery, requires a significant amount of courage and sensitivity. We will also delve into the intimate nature of words themselves. How do our words call into existence a new relational world? A new relationship? New persons? A final thread of this conversation focuses on experiencing

---

4 At times I choose to use the word *selfs* instead of selves, because I hope to maintain a focus as to how intimacy develops our sense of *self*. Exceptions to this will occur when I am clearly talking about group dynamics, such as, *themselves* or *ourselves*.

intimacy as art, aesthetics, and beauty. Here we will play with the idea that intimacy is achieved and experienced in the same way that works of art take effort and vulnerability and risk.

A Final Word of Hope ... and Caution

We are made for intimacy. But we all have developed coping strategies, some healthy and some not so healthy, to protect us from the potential hurt and pain that come when intimacy goes "wrong." Engaging the three conversations that comprise this book could potentially undo some of the ways you have been managing this part of your life. As such, maintain good social and psychological support while reading this book. I'm a big fan of counseling, keeping good friends, journaling, and understanding that our lives are part of something bigger than we fully understand.

As I mentioned previously, I've not written this book as the final word on intimacy. Rather, I hope to engage you in an *intimate space* that broadens how we all think about this critical aspect of our lives. As your perspective expands and changes, when safe and appropriate, it is important to invite your relational partners into the conversation.[5] Each of your close relationships is a unique intimacy expression—your own relationship art.[6] So guard against feeling frustrated with your partners and your relationships after reading each thread of conversation. Instead, think about how you and your partner might build intimacy in ways that work for you both.

Intimacy is risky business. But, therein lies the hope. Transforming your ideas about intimacy will change how you see yourself and how you see and relate to others. Intimacy at the most profound levels is central to our human experience and, as such, to our development as loving, caring persons. It is my hope that, as we engage these intimate conversations together, a new awareness will revolutionize our lives and the world in which we live.

Doug
Phoenix, AZ and Lake Ozonia, NY

---

5   When you're talking with your family, friends, and romantic partners about what you are learning and encountering in *Intimate Spaces*, you'll miss the point of the book and risk damaging your relationships if you try to tell them the "right" way to be intimate. Instead, invite them into a conversation where you mutually discover how this best plays out for the two of you.
6   The final thread of the book focuses on viewing relationships as works of art.

Conversation One

The Essence of Intimacy:
Discovery and Connection

Thread 1.1

When Relationships Become Intimate Spaces

Relationships—the joy and bane of our existence. We live and die by our relationships. When our relationships are good, life is good. When relationships are "working" our lives feel in sync, we find motivation to get up each morning. Alternatively, when things go wrong in our relationship world, life can feel hopeless, meaningless, dark, and heavy.[1]

To be a human being, is to be a relational being.

From conception, our human journey is a deeply relational one. In fact, "conception" itself is essentially relational. To conceive is to create, to imagine, to form—some "thing" suddenly exists that wasn't there a moment ago. The new life of a zygote. A fresh idea. Even understanding between partners—Flash! the light bulb goes on—I suddenly "get" what you are saying. And at the core of each of these expressions of conception is relationship. Sperm and egg unite. Old ideas clash with new contingencies and fresh ideas are born. Divergent human perspectives meet in a forest of words and ideas and suddenly find a third way to travel together.[2]

---

1 Douglas L. Kelley, Vincent R. Waldron, and Dayna N. Kloeber, *A Communicative Approach to Conflict, Forgiveness, and Reconciliation: Reimagining Our Relationships*, (New York: Routledge, 2019).
2 I discuss third way process in a recent article, Douglas L. Kelley, "Just Relationships: A Third Way Ethic," *The Atlantic Journal of Communication* (2019).

Relationship Spaces

A prominent Starfleet captain is noted as proclaiming, "Space. The final frontier."[3] And, indeed it is. Our inner relationship spaces are no less formidable frontiers to discover than is outer space. They are chockfull of possibilities waiting to be discovered. However, most of us don't intentionally explore our relationships until we are forced to. I think of a dear student of mine who took all of my relationship classes, but only after swearing off romantic relationships in the aftermath of three girlfriends in a row cheating on him. And my close friends who thought they had parenting figured out … until they adopted young twin girls and discovered that bonding and attachment with their new daughters was challenging new territory. Also, memorable, a friend who dined with me weekly during the time my wife and I were separated, once reflected, "You and Ann seem to be learning so much about one another and yourselves. Maybe my wife and I should try counseling."

My friend's desire to keep growing in his marriage was laudable, but relationship spaces are wild, unpredictable, dangerous, and should be engaged with expectation, excitement and … caution. As a mentor told me when I began doing some urban work in my college days, "I don't want you to be afraid, but I do want you to be smart." In the same way, we come to our relationships with eyes wide open to both positive and negative possibilities. When free to develop in healthy ways, our relationship spaces provide the rich soil and emotional fodder needed to grow into something we can scarcely imagine. In this vulnerable relational space we become ourselves—experiencing and expressing those parts of our "self" that we have been protecting and holding back. And, somewhat surprising, we then find ourselves free to more fully contribute to the lives of those for whom we care.

Relationship Spaces As Systems

Connections between persons are the essence of *relationship spaces*. One way to think about this is to picture a relationship space as a system. Social scientists have conceptualized relational systems as webs of connection between people. Notably, early work by psychologists Virginia Satir[4],

---

3 Gene Roddenberry, *Star Trek: The Original Series* (Hollywood, CA: NBC, 1969).
4 Virginia Satir, *Conjoint Family Therapy: A Guide to Theory and Technique* (Palo Alto: Science and Behavior Books, 1967).

Salvador Minuchin[5], and Watzlawick, Beavin, and Jackson[6] shifted emphasis away from "fixing" a "problem-individual" to focusing on the interactions between people. Fixing problem-individuals can sound something like: "If John would just stop drinking ..." or "We'll be okay when Mandy settles down and grows up." Statements like these assume that individuals are solely responsible for relationship problems—once the individual stops her or his "bad" behavior, everything should return to "normal." As true as it is that individuals need to take responsibility for the choices they make, much of the beauty and power of relationships is lost when we fail to see our relationship behavior as occurring within relational systems and, subsequently, fail to recognize that we can work together to change behavior and transform our relationships.[7]

Systems perspectives shift our relationship frames[8] from being focused on individual effort (two separate individuals each hoping to be relationally "good" enough) to focusing on collaboratively working together to co-create transformative relational spaces. It is in these spaces that we are able to find and express our sense of self. When something isn't "working" in the relationship, instead of it being the job of one individual to "fix the bad behavior", it is now deemed an opportunity for both partners to work together to change how the behavior functions within the relationship.[9] In the previous paragraph, John's drinking and Mandy's "acting out" may have been serving multiple functions, such as helping each of them feel accepted by their peers or manage stress. Unfortunately, those behaviors were also functioning to disrupt certain of their family and friendship relationships. When viewed from a systems perspective, rather than exhorting each of them to stop their "bad" behavior, relational partners work together to create new behavioral patterns that are healthy for everyone involved.

---

5   Salvador Minuchin, *Families and Family Therapy* (Cambridge: Harvard University Press. 1974).

6   Paul Watzlawick, Janet Beavin Bavelas, and Don D. Jackson, *Pragmatics of Human Communication: A Study of Interactional Patterns, Pathologies and Paradoxes* (New York: W.W. Norton & Company, 2011).

7   Throughout the book we will run into complex issues, such as these. It's important to recognize that while it is preferable to work together to solve relational problems, sometimes boundaries have to be set to protect oneself from destructive behavior (such as living with an abusive partner that refuses to get or receive help).

8   Relationship frames are guiding perspectives that frame, or influence, how we see our relationships (for more on this see: Douglas L. Kelley, *Just Relationships: Living Out Social Justice as Mentor, Family, Friend, and Lover* (New York: Routledge, 2017).

9   I tend to take a functional perspective in studying relationships. That is, I tend to focus more on how behavior is being used or what effect it has, than on the actual behavior itself. For instance, a slight touch on the arm can function (be used or interpreted) as a signal for control or for affection.

Three family systems theory concepts provide insight into the nature of our intimate spaces: interdependence, synergy, and resilience.[10] Family systems theorists view families as complex webs of *interdependent* connections between family members. An essential part of what it means to be in relationship is to have a sense of mutual dependence. The resultant tension between being an autonomous individual (self-sustaining and unconstrained by others' expectations and desires) and being appropriately dependent on others (depending on others to meet essential needs and to provide input as to how we are living) is a lifelong struggle for most of us and, as we will discuss shortly, a critical part of finding intimacy in our relationships.

Interdependence, and the resulting relational tension that it produces, often manifests as nonsummativity,[11] a *synergy* that is more than the sum of the parts and, correspondingly, creates something beyond what we might predict. This means that understanding our relationships is about much more than simply understanding each individual partner. Like a chemistry experiment, it's about understanding what happens when you combine two separate elements (partners) together. Remember making a simulated volcano eruption in science class by combining two seemingly benign elements: baking soda and vinegar? The focus shifts from the individual elements to the surprising outcome of their unique combination. Similarly, the dynamic mix of two individuals with different family and cultural backgrounds, personalities, and relationship pasts creates a synergism that produces new relational patterns that cannot fully be predicted. Some of these patterns are useful, even life-giving, while others tear at the very fabric of our relationships and sense of self.

To better get an idea of how synergy and nonsummativity affect one our relationships, consider your good friend, Cassie, for a moment. She's smart, reasonable, and playful. The synergy you experience when the two of you are together makes you feel brighter, more fun loving, more creative. One day you meet her mother and immediately like her. You can tell from where Cassie gets her personality. However, moments later Cassie and her mom (much to your surprise) are embroiled in a seemingly irrational argument, locked into

---

10 I have taken liberty in using the term resilience to describe systems' tendency to survive. For more on systems theory, find: Jody Koenig Kellas, "Communicated Narrative Sense-Making Theory: Linking Storytelling and Well-being," in *Engaging Theories in Family Communication: Multiple Perspectives*, eds. Dawn O. Braithwaite, Elizabeth A. Suter, and Kory Floyd (New York: Routledge, 2018), 62–74; Paul Watzlawick, Janet Beavin Bavelas, and Don D. Jackson, *Pragmatics of Human Communication: A Study of Interactional Patterns, Pathologies and Paradoxes* (New York: W.W. Norton & Company, 2011).

11 Nonsummativity essentially means that things don't add up as expected (non-sum). Usually you get more than you would expect ($2 + 2 = 5$).

their own ways of seeing to the point of being unkind to each other. What's happened? Synergy and nonsummativity—well-worn communication patterns feeding off of one another to such an extent that one-plus-one suddenly becomes three or four or five! Much more than expected. And, to reiterate, this synergistic effect can be for the good (like the synergy you experience in your friendship with Cassie), or for the not so good (like Cassie and her mom's rather habitual conflict episodes).[12]

Relational systems are also wonderfully *resilient*.[13] Resilience manifests in two ways, both of which involve adapting to change. First, systems are constantly working in order to maintain a degree of stability and ensure survival. In the same way that the human body's immune system attempts to regulate its temperature at approximately 37 degrees Celsius, our relationship spaces are largely characterized by habitual (mindless) communication patterns between partners that keep our relationships somewhat predictable and stable. I find it comforting and useful to know that in spite of all the new experiences my wife, Ann, and I encounter each day, our relationship will largely be the same when we arrive home at day's end as it was when we parted. On the other hand, when left unchecked, the tendency for systems to maintain stability can make it difficult to change destructive patterns of behavior (as we saw in the previous example with Cassie and her mother).

Thankfully, however, the second way relationship resilience shows up is in our ability to be responsive and adaptive to ever-changing circumstances. Healthy relationships tend to be wonderfully resilient as they continually adapt to changing contingencies, whereas less healthy relationships are characterized by rigid (predictable, unchanging) patterns of behavior. Hopefully, Cassie and her mom will eventually modify their behavior patterns in ways that bring new life to them both.

---

12 *Threads* 1.3 and 1.7 use "third way" process to describe the phenomenon that something creative and, to some degree, unexpected comes out of these relational tensions.

13 Patrice M. Buzzanell, "Resilience: Talking, Resisting, and Imagining New Normalcies into Being," *Journal of Communication* 60, no. 1 (March 2010): 1–14, https://doi.org/10.1111/j.1460-2466.2009.01469.x; Patrice M. Buzzanell and Lynn H. Turner, "Emotion Work Revealed by Job Loss Discourse: Backgrounding-Foregrounding of Feelings, Construction of Normalcy, and (Re)instituting of Traditional Masculinities," *Journal of Applied Communication Research* 31, no 1. (2003): 27–57, https://doi.org/10.1080/00909880305375.

> ## Growing Close 1.1.1
>
> Take a minute to think about two relationships that are important to you. How are these relationship spaces each unique in terms of interdependence, synergy, and resilient patterns? Do these unique patterns have positive or negative effects on your relationship or you and your partners' sense of self? In light of your responses, think about how you behave differently in each of these relationship spaces?

Inter "Personal" Relationships

Archbishop Desmond Tutu, of South Africa, though not formally a systems theorist, has spent much of his adult life healing relationship systems in the aftermath of Apartheid. In this regard, Tutu has offered the concept of, *Ubuntu,* to help us see people as intricately related, emerging as part of an ever-evolving human collective. Tutu beautifully describes the South African concept of *Ubuntu* as follows: "My humanity is caught up, is inextricably bound up, in yours. ... A person is a person through other persons. ... I am human because I belong. I participate. I share."[14] *Ubuntu* reveals relationships as spaces where we become more than people, we become *persons.*

Person is an important word for me. We become persons as we interact with others in ways that recognize our inner humanness. Philosopher Martin Buber, in his classic work, I and Thou, tells us, "Persons appear by entering into relation with other persons."[15] In essence, for Buber, we become persons when we relate to others as I-You, rather than I-It. I-It relating is characterized by distance between self and other, treating relationship partners as objects. Often, this takes the form of seeing others primarily in terms of standard roles (e.g., teacher, doctor, police officer, or child, parent, romantic partner) or group identification (e.g., military, religion, race, culture, age, sexual identity). By contrast, I-You relating requires one's whole being and recognition of and connection with the uniqueness of the "other." This distinction will be fundamental for us as we explore the nature of intimate relationships.

---

14 Desmond Tutu, *No Future Without Forgiveness* (New York, NY: Doubleday, 1999), 31.
15 Martin Buber, *I and Thou,* trans. Walter Kaufmann (New York: Charles Scribner's Sons, 1970), 57.

Based on Buber's thinking, communication scholar, John Stewart, offers five communication elements that characterize how we can transform our interactions into inter- "personal" encounters.[16] That is, when we enact these elements we move beyond reacting to people solely based on their role or group-based characteristics, to interacting with them based on their individual, personal identities. According to Stewart, we recognize others as persons when we treat them as being unique, unmeasurable, responsive, reflective, and addressable. In other words, I treat you as a person when my behavior recognizes your uniqueness (being male doesn't mean you don't cry; as a friend, you aren't interchangeable as if switching out a pair of AA batteries) and complexity (I can't understand you simply by measuring and labeling your Myers–Briggs personality type), your ability to make choices (you have ideas, a voice, and are capable of responding to an ever-changing environment) and reflect on those choices (you wonder if the way you spoke to me sounded harsh), and that I can talk with you not at you (I engage you in a dialogue, rather than a monologue).

Growing Close 1.1.2

To get a hold of what it means to treat others as persons, think about your own relational experience. To what extent have your parents, a close friend, or a romantic partner ...

- Recognized you as unique and irreplaceable?
- Avoided the temptation to measure you by putting you in a "box" (this often happens through labeling—"He's the baby" or "He's my dorky friend")?[7]
- Given you opportunity to make your own choices?
- Respected your ability to reflect on life by engaging you in adult-like discussion?
- Talk *with* you rather than *at* you?

---

16   John Stewart, *Bridges Not Walls: A Book about Interpersonal Communication*, 11th ed. (New York: McGraw-Hill, 2012), 14–41.
17   Note that labeling is tricky. Some individuals embrace labels, such as being the "baby", in ways that help them feel connected, whereas others feel constricted by them. One must also realize that how he or she feels about being labeled may change with age.

Personal vs. Social Relationships

In contrast to the personal treatment of others, social relationships are primarily based on roles that each person plays, such as doctor–patient, cashier–customer, and employer–employee. Very little of our "unique person" is evident to others when our relationships are primarily based on roles. That said, maintaining certain relationships as social, not personal, is often prudent as we may have neither the time, energy, or desire to escalate the relationship (for example, you may not feel the need to know your mortgage broker or garage mechanic personally). What is important to recognize is that, for whatever reasons we choose to do so, relating to others exclusively according to their social roles limits the opportunity for intimacy in those relationships.

Early work by researchers Mark Knapp, Donald Ellis, and Barbara Williams[18] brings to light key differences between personal and social relationships. Although the study has been around for awhile, I find their conclusions have held up over time and make practical sense. Surveying more than 1000 participants across the United States, they found close relationships to be characterized by more personalized communication (*depth*), such as sharing private information and feelings, developing unique meanings and ways of sharing those meanings, and even being willing to judge one another (for example, I count on my closest friends to tell me when I'm out of line). In this way, personal relationships move beyond role enactment and, instead, risk engaging the "person."

Knapp and colleagues also found *synchronized* communication to be associated with intimate relationships. Synchronous conversations seem effortless, spontaneous, relaxed, and smooth-flowing. Think about the times when you were interacting with someone and the two of you seemed "in sync" or the conversation just "clicked." This type of synchronization engenders a nearly immediate sense of liking and connection. Interestingly, there is often an informality to these kinds of interactions, as formal norms tend to inhibit spontaneous, synchronized responses.

I'm thinking right now of the first time I met Dick, who became my closest friend. Our wives had connected through a local church and arranged for the four of us to meet for dinner. The meal was characterized by lively conversation, including a discussion of favorite childhood cartoons. When Bugs Bunny's nemesis, the Tasmanian Devil, was mentioned, Dick and I

---

18   Mark L. Knapp, Donald G. Ellis, and Barbara A. Williams, "Perceptions of Communication Behavior Associated with Relationship Terms," *Communications Monographs* 47, no. 4 (1980): 262–278, https://doi.org/10.1080/03637758009376036.

Growing Close 1.1.3

The last few pages have introduced a number of new thoughts about personal relationships. To pull these all together, take a moment to consider three of your valued relationships that are distinctively different from one another. Don't limit yourself to romantic relationships. Think of how these three relationships vary in terms of interdependence, synergy, resilience, depth, synchronicity, and each partner being recognized and treated as a person. Now, look for what these relationships might hold in common. How might this exercise help you recognize what is present in a relationship when it is really "working" for you?

---

spontaneously turned to one another and imitated the devil's signature grunting and growling sounds. There was a pause, followed by great laughter. We were in sync! And, in that moment, we both knew that we were going to be great friends.[19]

Reclaiming Relationship Terms

Western culture has confused relationship matters in its use of certain terms, a couple of which I hope to reclaim for our intimacy discussions. A quick tour of the Internet confirms that "being in a relationship" generally refers to romantic affiliations. If someone at work asks, "Are you in a relationship?" you would likely not reply, "Actually, I have several good friends," or "My son and I are close." You might say something like, "I've been dating someone regularly for the past two months," or "No, I haven't been seeing anyone lately." Of interest to me is that, while the term "relationship" has been coopted to represent romantic endeavors, actually family and friend relationships may exhibit much more of what we really mean when we think about being in a relationship – understanding, trust, safety, enjoyment.

---

19 That moment was so significant that over the years we often gave one another Tasmanian Devil gifts. As I write these words, I am looking at a Tasmanian Devil light hanging on my wall—a gift I gave to Dick and that was returned to me upon his death seven years ago.

As such, when I use the term relationship, I am referring to close connection between persons, whether they be family, friends, or lovers.

Likewise, the term *partner* has come to be understood as unmarried, romantic relations, in particular, cohabitation.[20] Yet, I consider my wife, my partner. I consider both my sons to be relational partners. My daughters-in-law? You got it—partners. What about my close friends? Yup, partners. I consider partners to be equals who collaboratively negotiate (verbally or nonverbally) their relationship dynamics for the long haul. As such, throughout *Intimate Spaces* when I use the term *partner* or *relational partner* I am referring to any individual engaged in a long-term, personal relationship—family, friend, lover.

Intimate Reflections

As we finish this thread of our first conversation, take a moment to reflect on our discussion thus far. We have been considering close relationships as spaces characterized by interdependence, synergy, resilience, depth, synchronicity, and each partner being recognized and treated as a person. In particular, how might viewing relationships as spaces that reveal people as *persons* change your perspective, choices, or behavior in your relationships? For instance, would it have an impact on how you think about dating, maintaining long-term relationships, or parenting? What would it mean to begin viewing your current relational partners as persons? Or other persons as potential relational partners? How might viewing a sexual partner as a person and relational partner change your sexual experience? How might your past relationship experiences and anticipated relational futures influence how you communicate in long-term relationships?

The following threads to this first conversation more fully explore these questions. Next is a short reflection suggesting that we are *made for intimacy.* If true, how might that change the way you prioritize relationships in your life?

---

20 Douglas L. Kelley, *Marital Communication* (Cambridge, England: Polity Press, 2012).

Thread 1.2

Made for Intimacy

Let him kiss me with the kisses of his mouth!
For your love is better than wine ...
Let us run!

—Song of Songs[1]

The data obtained "make it obvious that contact comfort is a variable of overwhelming importance in the development of affectional responses, whereas lactation is a variable of negligible importance"[2]

—Harry F. Harlow

Sources as diverse as the Song of Songs from Hebrew scriptures and the classic Harlow monkey studies from modern psychology provide insight into human beings' need for intimacy.[3] Ancient literature is strewn with what could pass as modern day relationship struggles—human beings and gods in rapture or in conflict over family, friends, and persons of desire. Likewise, modern science has long been interested in the seeming mythic power of intimate, loving

---

1 Song of Solomon 8:7 English Standard Version.
2 Harry F. Harlow, "The Nature of Love," *American Psychologist* 13, no. 12 (1958): 673, http://dx.doi.org/10.1037/h0047884.
3 Interesting authors regarding these topics include Joseph Campbell (*The Power of Myth*), Robert Bly (*Iron John*), and various writings by Freud and Jung.

relationships. Here we consider our need for intimacy as something that extends far beyond desire, passion, or simple pleasure. Perhaps we are, indeed, made for intimacy.

Relationally Made

Human development is relational by nature. My college biology professor, Dr. Trout (I'm not making that up),[4] was fond of saying, you begin your human journey in a "womb without a view." True. But it turns out that this windowless womb is a relational one. In *Thread 1.1* we discussed the tendency for adult relational partners to synchronize their behaviors, but as it turns out, prenatal, mother and child are already doing this very thing.[5] And other physiological phenomena, like the hormone oxytocin, encourage attachment between child and parent,[6] influencing our early development as relational creatures.

Attachment to parents or other caregivers continues to be facilitated through adolescence. There are a few mammalian species that take longer to grow up than we do, but we rank toward the top when it comes to length of time needed before a child can survive independently of her or his guardians. This means that key childhood and adolescent development occurs within a relationship context. Consider the relational meaning embedded in how we learn motor skills ("That a girl. You can do it! Come to Daddy."), language ("Say ma ..... ma, ma ... ma, mama!"),[7] and develop cognitive and moral skills associated with our ability to see the perspective of others ("Treat others as you would have others treat you," "How do you think your friend feels about what you did?").[8]

---

4 Dr. Trout taught biology at Phoenix College in the 70s. He was one of my favorite professors.

5 Janet A. DiPietro, Laura E. Caulfield, Rafael A. Irizarry, Ping Chen, Mario Merialdi, et al., "Prenatal Development of Intrafetal and Maternal-Fetal Synchrony," *Behavioral Neuroscience* 120 (2006): 687–701, DOI:10.1037/0735-7044.120.3.687

6 Ruth Feldman and Marian J. Bakermans-Kranenburg, "Oxytocin: A Parenting Hormone," *Current Opinion in Psychology* 15, (2017): 13–18, https://doi.org/10.1016/j.copsyc.2017.02.011.

7 Jana M. Iverson, "Developing Language in a Developing Body: The Relationship Between Motor Development and Language Development," *Journal of Child Language* 37, no. 2 (2010): 229–61, https://doi.org/10.1017/S0305000909990432.

8 Vincent R. Waldron et al., "How Parents Communicate Right and Wrong: A Study of Memorable Moral Messages Recalled by Emerging Adults," *Journal of Family* Communication 14, no. 4 (2014): 374–97, https://doi.org/10.1080/15267431.2014.946032.

Growing Close 1.2.1

Based on this brief discussion, think about how relationships have affected your life. How were relationships valued in the home in which you grew up? How have you responded to that upbringing? Have you found yourself yearning for relationship or preferring to find your own way? Do you think the way in which you value relationships is healthy? Could it use some tweaking?

Before reading the next section, ask the same questions regarding touch. How was touch expressed in your family of origin? What about in your adult life? Are you a "touchy" person, preferring to touch and be touched, or do you like your own space? Of course, those distinctions are quite general. You might enjoy touch from some people, but not others, or might be predisposed to certain kinds of touch, but not others. The key is to recognize how each of us has used and responded to touch throughout our lives. Read on to continue thinking about the critical role touch plays in our human experience.

Human Touch and Affection

A significant aspect of our relational human development is the role touch and affection play in our desire for human connection. An early social scientific look at these elements came from Harlow's (1958) classic experiment (watched by many of us in *Introduction to Psychology* during our first year in college) wherein researchers provided rhesus monkey infants the option of being with surrogate mothers: one made up of wire provided with a bottle for nursing, the other made up of cloth equipped with a heat lamp for warmth. Harlow (1958) describes:

> We were not surprised to discover that contact comfort was an important basic affectional or love variable, but we did not expect it to overshadow so completely the variable of nursing; indeed, the disparity is so great as to suggest that the primary function of nursing as an affectional variable

is that of insuring frequent and intimate body contact of the infant with the mother. Certainly man cannot live by milk alone. (p. 677)

Certainly! Harlow's program of study, while limited in certain conclusions, stimulated important thinking regarding touch and mammalian development. Recent research has demonstrated that nurturing children through touch is actually beneficial for social breain development.[9] And, more than that, a current overview of research has concluded that affectionate touch promotes relational, psychological, and physical well-being for adults, as well.[10] Oh, and good news for those of you who like to pucker up! Scientists have linked romantic kissing to improvements in perceived stress, relationship satisfaction, and even total serum cholesterol levels.[11]

The kissing research was conducted by communication researcher, Kory Floyd, who has posed *Affection Exchange Theory* (AET) as one way of understanding the function of affectionate touch in human relationships.[12] Floyd highlights that the need and capacity for affection are inborn. Essentially, as human beings we are "naturally" attracted to relationships that feel safe and warm. And, further, affectionate communication promotes significant, long-term relationships that allow for shared resources and provide means of evaluating whether an individual is a potential viable partner or parent. In other words, affectionate communication is essential to our physical and psychological/emotional survival.

Intimate Reflections

One of the longest longitudinal studies on record, the Harvard Study of Adult Development, has been following men (and eventually their wives) since

9 Ilona Croy et al., "Gentle Touch Perception: From Early Childhood to Adolescence," *Developmental Cognitive Neuroscience* 35, (2019): 81-86, https://doi:10.1016/j.dcn.2017.07.009; Rima Shore, *Rethinking the Brain: New Insights into Early Development* (New York: Families and Work Institute, 1997).

10 Brittany Jakubiak and Brooke C. Feeney, "Affectionate Touch to Promote Relational, Psychological, and Physical Well-Being in Adulthood: A Theoretical Model and Review of the Research," *Personality and Social Psychology Review* 21, no. 3 (2017): 228–52, https://doi.org/10.1177/1088868316650307.

11 Kory Floyd et al., "Kissing in Marital and Cohabiting Relationships: Effects on Blood Lipids, Stress, and Relationship Satisfaction," *Western Journal of Communication* 73, no. 2 (2009): 113–33, http://dx.doi.org/10.1080/10570310902856071.

12 Kory Floyd, "Human Affection Exchange: V. Attributes of the Highly Affectionate," *Communication Quarterly* 50, no. 2 (2002): 135–52, https://doi.org/10.1080/01463370209385653.

Growing Close 1.2.2

Take a moment to consider this brief discussion about the innate and essential role affection plays in our human development. What if affection, closeness, belonging, and intimacy are all integral to our survival and development as persons? How does this change your view of intimacy? Affection? Touch? Might this make a difference as to how you think about maintaining close relationships in your life?

1938. After 80 years of data collection, what have they learned? Ponder this statement regarding the importance of relationships in our lives:

> *Close relationships, more than money or fame, are what keep people happy throughout their lives, the study revealed. Those ties protect people from life's discontents, help to delay mental and physical decline, and are better predictors of long and happy lives than social class, IQ, or even genes.*[13]

It is clear that human relationships are central to our well-being, especially when they facilitate a sense of belonging and intimacy.[14] But, how do we manage the emotional risk that comes with intimacy and connection? Perhaps your experience has been much like that of Dr. Meredith Grey: "Intimacy is a four-syllable word for 'Here are my heart and soul, please grind them into hamburger and enjoy.'"[15] The following conversational thread, *The Struggle for Connection and Autonomy*, explores the paradoxical tensions we experience as we negotiate closedness and openness, and autonomy and connection, in our personal relationships. And, as we invite others to safely "co-own" our relational lives.

---

13 Liz Mineo, "Good Genes Are Nice, But Joy is Better," *The Harvard Gazette*, accessed June 22, 2019, https://news.harvard.edu/gazette/story/2017/04/over-nearly-80-years-harvard-study-has-been-showing-how-to-live-a-healthy-and-happy-life/.

14 Lisa F. Berkman, "The Role of Social Relations in Health Promotion," *Psychosomatic Medicine* 57, no. 3 (1995): 245–54.

15 *Grey's Anatomy*, season 1, episode 4, "No Man's Land," directed by Adam Davidson and written by James D. Parriott, aired April 17, 2005, ABC.

Thread 1.3

The Struggle for Connection and Autonomy

ade for intimacy? Absolutely. But that doesn't mean that intimacy comes easily. Most people find that creating and maintaining intimacy is a struggle. In fact, this struggle is a core characteristic of close personal relationships. If that sounds disheartening, don't worry, the upside is that healthy struggle is at the core of creating intimacy and growing more deeply as individuals. Struggle can take many forms, but here I am referring to a deep level of tension that is always present as we negotiate our personal relationships. Although we may not always be aware of it, we are constantly being pulled between seemingly opposite forces. Consider Alejandra's description of her dating patterns:

> *Typically I flirt with a guy I like until he is clearly interested. Then we start hanging out together. Within a couple weeks we become an item. It's all good. We're enjoying each other and things couldn't be better. Then, two to three months in, I dump him. It's always a shock to the guy because things are so good. I'm not sure why I do it. Maybe I just don't want to get hurt first, but something inside of me just needs to get out. Afterwards, I hang out with my friends, including guys, and eventually start flirting, and it all starts over again.*

Alejandra is experiencing the tension between wanting connection with others, but at the same time not wanting to be constrained by the limitations inherent in all relationships. In this third thread of our first conversation, we begin to explore intimacy basics by discussing how the strain between autonomy and connection, and privacy (closedness) and openness, creates space for intimacy to emerge—something I call *third way* process.

A Relationship Primer

The 1970s witnessed a flurry of social scientific research focusing on personal relationships. Social Penetration Theory, developed by psychologists Irwin Altman and Dalmas Taylor, provided a significant contribution to the way we think about relationships and, as you'll come to find out, has continued to influence our thinking today.[1] The basic idea is that intimacy increases as relational partners' communication grows in breadth (the number of facets of one's life considered appropriate to discuss or reveal) and depth (the amount of detail you reveal about each facet). Like peeling away layers of an onion (the theory is more popularly referred to as Onion Skin Theory), intimacy develops as each partner provides *access* to himself or herself through broad and deep communication. Social penetration occurs as individuals penetrate their partner's public persona and reach the inner person. I've always thought the onion analogy was particularly fitting, because the deeper you go into onions and relationships the more crying you do!

Altman and Taylor described this access-gaining process as moving through four stages. *Orientation* is the rudimentary process of meeting someone and determining whether or not you think the relationship has potential to go deeper.

Exploratory affective exchange and affective exchange represent the next two stages whereby individuals share more deeply and broadly, and test the relationship's ability to accept and sustain the sharing of affect. Think of *affect* as the positive or negative feelings and emotions you experience (note the root of *affection* is *affect*) and affective exchange as the sharing of or exposure to those feelings and emotions, either verbally or nonverbally.[2] This affective exposure might be direct and intentional ("I'm angry with you" stated with tense vocal

---

1 Irwin Altman and Dalmas A. Taylor, *Social Penetration Theory: The Development of Interpersonal Relationships* (New York: Holt, Rinehart & Winston, 1973).

2 Laura K. Guerrero, Peter A. Andersen, and Melanie R. Trost, "Communication and Emotion: Basic Concepts and Approaches," in *Handbook of Communication and Emotion: Research, Theory, Application, and Contexts*, eds. Peter A. Andersen & Laura K. Guerrero (San Diego, CA: Academic Press, 1996), 3–27.

characteristics) or leaked and unintentional (as your partner tells you she is leaving, your eyes well up with tears) or some combination of these elements.

The final stage, *stable exchange*, represents a steady state where sharing of information and affect happens regularly (although, interestingly enough, explicit sharing may happen less often than in the previous stages that are often characterized by more rapid growth).

Growing Close 1.3.1

One of the reasons I am drawn to *Social Penetration Theory* is that I've come to appreciate the significant role emotions and feelings play in our close relationships. The deepest part of the onion, our inner-self, is populated by deep emotional responses, such as the hopes and fears that often leave us feeling vulnerable.[3]

Take a moment to consider two different responses to a conversation with John.

- "John shared detailed information with me today. I've analyzed his situation and believe he is in trouble."

- "John really opened up to me today. It means a lot that he would share with me and I'm really worried that he is in trouble."

The first response sounds a bit sterile—it recognizes that John is in trouble, but is distant, personally unaffected by the information shared. There appears to be little affective exchange. In contrast, the second response goes deeper by recognizing the relational implications of the John's sharing, along with the fact that he may need help.

How has affect (feelings and emotions) affected your relationship experience? Remember that feelings don't have to be expressed to have an effect on you. In fact, suppressed emotions can have a substantial impact on your behavior.

---

3 Although there is scientific debate about what an emotion is, many social scientists think of emotion as feelings, plus cognition about those feelings. For instance, you can experience something as negative and intense, but to some extent it is your thinking related to these feelings that tells you whether you are sad or angry.

Communication researcher Mark Knapp expanded Altman and Taylor's stages, placing an emphasis on communication behavior. Knapp's five *Coming Together* stages[4] can be briefly characterized as follows: *initiation*, greeting behavior or the nod of recognition you give to someone that you notice on a regular basis, but otherwise with whom you seldom interact; *experimenting*, small talk, which can include auditioning to gauge the potential for a deeper relationship; *intensifying*, increase in self-disclosure and nonverbal immediacy, such as positive facial expressions, close proximity, and affectionate touch; *integrating*, sustained experience of intensifying behaviors along with integration of one's social networks, life rhythms, and identity; *bonding*, public displays of the relationship commitment, such as marriage, buying a house, or having a child.

As you read through these stages, you are likely thinking through the stages of your own relationships—"My friendship with Brad has definitely integrated, but my relatively new dating relationship is somewhere between experimenting or early intensifying." However, one limitation of this approach to understanding relationship development is that stages imply a linear progression toward intimacy. And, even though stage-based models often highlight that relationships can skip stages, go backward, or stabilize at various stages, the language embedded within the models (e.g., "going backwards," "skipping") implies that all relationships are headed toward intimacy, unless they get derailed.[5]

In reality there are various relationship types with various expectations for intimacy or closeness. You may be quite satisfied with the casual, feel-good vibe you share with the server at your favorite cafe. Or you might be the type that is content with one or two good friends while the rest of your relationships are somewhat perfunctory. Or you might even be like my wife, Ann, and care very little for small talk, preferring instead to jump straight into deep subjects, even with new acquaintances.

Besides the various permutations as to how we enact our connections with others, relationships are messy! For instance, you might feel close to someone in certain ways, but not in others. Your friend, Josh, is easy to talk to, but awkward to just hang out with. You are attracted to Maria, but are cautious because you don't trust her. This makes it difficult to track relationships

---

4   Mark L. Knapp, *Interpersonal Communication and Human Relationships* (Boston: Allyn & Bacon, 1984); Mark L. Knapp, Anita L. Vangelisti and John P. Caughlin, *Interpersonal Communication and Human Relationships*, 7th ed. (Boston: Allyn & Bacon/Pearson, 2013).

5   The tendency to see linear progression is common. Vince Waldron and I have created a model representing the forgiveness process, *Communication Tasks of Forgiveness*. We intentionally avoided the word "stages" and used "tasks" to circumvent creating a sense of linear progression, but multiple times I have heard individuals refer to our tasks in a linear way—"You start with identifying the transgression, followed my managing emotions ... ."

in a linear manner. That is, classic intimacy markers (more time, touch, and talk) don't always lead to more closeness. This messiness makes it difficult to know when you are making "progress" in the relationship – think about the rocky dating relationships that so many of us have had—like a kitchen light switch we are: on–off, on–off, on–off, on–dim ("Are we on or are we off?!").

Relational Tension and Paradox

Stage-based approaches to understanding relationship processes are intuitively appealing ("We're an item!" or "We've been stuck at this stage for a long time. It's time to commit or move on!"), but as we have seen also have certain limitations. One additional limitation occurs when we view relationships, within any given stage, as stable and unchanging. In such cases, when things go "wrong," we can find ourselves lamenting that we can't get our relationship back to "normal," back to feeling like it did, back to the stage we were at. And while these sentiments are certainly understandable, and even warranted at times, there is real danger that clinging to the past will blind us to the dynamic, ever-changing nature of our relationships and, as such, inhibit potential future growth.[6]

An alternative to viewing relationships as developing through stages, is to take a dialectical approach that focuses on the ever-present tensions and struggles within personal relationships. *Relational Dialectics Theory*[7] provides a dynamic lens with which to view the vibrant nature of our relationships.[8]

To understand this perspective, let's start with the idea of discourse. A discourse, in the broadest sense of the word, is a system of beliefs that gives meaning to a particular statement. Notably, we are often unaware of the larger discourses represented by our statements. For example, in the United States, the song, *My Way*, written by Paul Anka and popularized by Frank Sinatra, represents a common discourse of individualism (Americans tend to value

---

6 In another project I just completed, my co-authors and I debunk the idea that we can go back to "normal," preferring instead to think about how we can *reimagine our relationships.* That said, as we discussed in *Thread 1.1*, relational systems work to maintain some stability to ensure survival; Douglas L. Kelley, Vincent R. Waldron, and Dayna N. Kloeber, *A Communicative Approach to Conflict, Forgiveness, and Reconciliation: Reimagining Our Relationships*, (New York: Routledge, 2019).

7 Leslie A. Baxter, "Relational Dialectics Theory: Multivocal Dialogues of Family Communication," in *Engaging Theories in Family Communication: Multiple Perspectives*, eds. Dawn O. Braithwaite and Leslie A. Baxter (Thousand Oaks, CA: SAGE, 2006), 130–45.

8 Elizabeth A. Suter and Leah M. Seurer, "Relational Dialectics Theory: Realizing the Dialogic Potential of Family Communication," in *Engaging Theories in Family Communication: Multiple Perspectives*, eds. Dawn O. Braithwaite, Elizabeth A. Suter, and Kory Floyd (New York, NY: Routledge, 2018), 62–74.

stories of people who "make it on their own"). On the other hand, Tom Cruise's famous line in Jerry McGuire, "You complete me," represents a broader discourse of romantic love that suggests true love is being completed by your relational partner (more to say on that in the second conversation of this book).

Dialectical tension is the struggle we experience to find meaning in competing discourses, such as these. For instance, individualism and romantic love are built on beliefs about autonomy and connection that often seem at odds with one another—I want to feel "completed" by being close to you, but I also want to maintain my independence and do it "my way." A common means of handling this struggle is to emphasize one part of the dialectic at a time - "Let's get away together this weekend, because I'm going to focus on work all next week." Here we see that one part of the dialectic is never completely without the other—the timing for getting away together (connection) is predicated on the impending need to work (autonomy). In this way, competing dialogues can be viewed as essential to one another (both/ and), rather than independent entities (either/or). That is, rather than focusing on either connection or autonomy, we recognize that both connection and autonomy are implicit in any discourse that concerns one or the other.

Consider the question and statement, "Will you marry me? I want to spend the rest of my life with you." These clearly focus on discourse related to romantic love and connection. However, they also have unmistakable implications regarding autonomy, which will inevitably have to be negotiated by the "happy couple." You simply cannot understand autonomy without connection (and vice versa). In a rather stunning example of this, a friend of mine who married later in life, found himself only living occasionally with his new wife. He had assumed marriage meant connection by living in a common household, whereas she had a much more independent idea of what it meant to connect. Today he is remarried to a woman who likes waking up next to him, and he rather playfully refers to the first marriage as "the marriage that never was."

PARADOX

It has been helpful for me to view the dialectical process through one of my favorite relational lenses—paradox. A paradox is a seemingly self-contradictory statement. Each element of the statement is equally true and, when held together, offers insight that can't be gained through either element alone. In *Thread 1.1*, I alluded to a *third way* process wherein the meeting of two seemingly contradictory truths gives birth to an even grander truth. This is the essence of paradox. Imagine your romantic partner tells you the following, "I love you and want to be close to you, but I need space." It would be easy to hear this challenging statement as nonsensical, "I want

Growing Close 1.3.2

How do you experience the struggles and tensions in your relationships? Are they primarily frustrating or are you able to appreciate the "truth" embedded in the two seemingly opposite perspectives of, "I want to be close to you" *and* "I need my space." Personally, I have been working on *living out the contradictions* in my life.[9] For example, a few years ago a counselor pointed out my resistance to anything that feels constricting, which is in sharp contrast to the anxiety and loneliness I feel when afforded too much freedom. To be honest, I have spent too much time trying to resolve these competing desires, rather than looking for new truth waiting to be born in my life through acceptance of both sides of this dialectical tension. In this particular struggle I finally realized and accepted the paradoxical truth that my healthy relationships, which are constricting in certain ways, provide the inner strength for me to live with more freedom, while on the other hand, the freedom I experience makes me a less needy and more interesting relationship partner. Turns out the pull between constriction and freedom actually creates some wonderfully intimate moments with my relational partners.

Is there a relational dialectic, or struggle, in one of your relationships that you can embrace and grow into? Is there a way you can begin to live out the contradiction rather than try to squelch it?[10]

to be connected to you" vs. "I don't want to be connected to you." And a natural response would be hurt and frustration, "Look, do you want to be with me, or not?"

---

9 Thanks to Parker Palmer's, *The Promise of Paradox*, for this phrase: Parker J. Palmer, *The Promise of Paradox: A Celebration of Contradictions in the Christian Life*, (Hoboken, NJ:John Wiley & Sons, 2010).

10 As I note in the preceding example, it often takes others to help us find ways to live out the contradiction.

A paradoxical perspective helps us view this struggle between discourses as a natural part of relationship life and to look for a larger truth that transcends the apparent contradiction. In the previous case, we embrace the fact that we need both connection and autonomy, ("I love you and want to be close to you, but I need space") and, hopefully, recognize the paradoxical truth that intimacy actually emerges from two *autonomous* individuals wanting *to connect*. For me, this is a much more compelling view of intimate relating than one that understands intimacy as some kind of "perfect compatibility" that feels easy (e.g., "We've never had a conflict"). In fact, you'll discover this relational "truth" (intimacy emerges from the paradoxical tension between autonomy and connection) surfacing in a number of conversational threads throughout *Intimate Spaces*.[11]

Privacy

I want to finish this conversational thread by examining a common relational tension that provides unique insights into intimacy – the pull between sharing something with others (openness) and keeping that same something private (closedness). This openness–closedness dialectic determines who we allow to see, hear, or experience our innermost thoughts and emotions, or as we discussed previously, with whom we can peel our private onions. As such, negotiating openness and closedness helps us determine what it means to be intimate.

Communication scholar, Sandra Petronio, has created an impressive program of research exploring the relational impact of privacy.[12] In *Communication Privacy Management Theory*, Petronio describes the dialectical nature of privacy—I want to share something with you (openness), but I also have a desire to protect myself by holding on to my private information (closedness). For example, you might struggle with the choice between feeling connected to your best friend by sharing honestly, and keeping your information private in order to avoid rejection. Paradoxically, the connection you are looking for is embedded in the relational risk of sharing—in fact, it is often the risk that causes partners to feel more intimate.

---

11 For more on *third way* process and paradox, see a recent article of mine: Douglas L. Kelley, "Just Relationships: A Third Way Ethic," *The Atlantic Journal of Communication* (2020).

12 Sandra Petronio, "Communication Boundary Management: A Theoretical Model of Managing Disclosure of Private Information Between Marital Couples," *Communication Theory* 1, no. 4 (1991): 311–35, https://doi.org/10.1111/j.1468-2885.1991.tb00023.x; Sandra Petronio, *Boundaries of Privacy: Dialectics of Disclosure* (Albany, NY: State University of New York Press, 2002).

Petronio describes this process as one of determining ownership. In essence, individuals consider private information to be something they own. This is why we may feel a sense of violation when others know details about us that we haven't chosen to reveal. And why we often keep information private in order to protect ourselves or to maintain a relationship at a particular level of closeness. For example, you may choose not to tell a casual friend that your dog just died because you are afraid that revealing your feelings will be misinterpreted by the friend as increasing the closeness of the relationship. On the flip side, you might choose to share about your dog's passing as a means of "testing the waters" to determine if the relationship is ready to go deeper.

Once we choose to share information with another individual, a privacy relationship is established and we negotiate what it means to *co-own* the information that has been shared. In essence, if I am willing to receive what you share with me, I now co-own that information and share the responsibility and privilege of owning it. This can bring growth and strengthening of the

Growing Close 1.3.3

Take a moment to think about autonomy and connection in your own life and in the lives of those you are close to. Do you tend to stay on one side of the autonomy—connection continuum?

Some people primarily play for fun and connection, while others play to compete and win. Some chiefly work to achieve goals, while others like the stimulation of working together. Some principally drink to connect, others to escape. For some, sports and sex are typically solitary acts even though others are involved, for others sports and sex involve collaboration and teamwork. And, similarly, some mainly use privacy to escape and avoid risk, whereas others use privacy as a means to connect by sharing the responsibilities and privileges of co-owning parts of one another's lives.

How do you tend to work out the autonomy—connection tension in your life? (Remember, connection and autonomy are deeply intertwined, one is not better than the other.)

relationship as we gain deeper access to one another. But, also this creates potential struggles for each partner. Most central for the disclosing partner is connection and trust: "I want to share this revelation to be connected with you, but can I trust you to handle this as I would?" And for the receiving partner, connection and responsibility are impending issues, "I'm thankful you shared this with me, but do I want to receive this information and be responsible for it?" Imagine your sister calling you and saying, "I'm going to tell you something, but you can't tell mom and dad." For both you and your sister this could be a sign of increased closeness, but she also has to determine if she trusts you enough to tell you, and you must decide whether you want the responsibility of abiding by her privacy rules.

Evident at this point is that co-owning is very much related to how we negotiate intimacy. Co-owning information in our personal relationships is an intimacy process whereby we negotiate the tension between openness and closedness and, consequently, between connection and autonomy. In this way, co-owning highlights for us the essential relationship paradox:

Intimacy emerges as autonomous partners struggle to connect.

Intimate Reflections

In this thread we have discussed how relationships move toward intimacy by going broad and deep (breadth and depth). At the same time, it has become clear that relationship development is not a linear, step-by-step process. It is messy and involves struggle between various relationship tensions, especially openness—closedness and connection—autonomy.

To finish this thread, let me share something of Ann's and my experience negotiating these relationship tensions. Our family affectionately refers to Ann as a social introvert. The social part of her values relationship and is very comfortable interacting with people. In contrast, the introverted part of her is determinedly independent and emotionally drained by being with people. This last year, when I asked what she wanted for her birthday, her initial reply was, "Time alone." *Whaaaat?!* As an only child I learned to be alone and to enjoy it. But my only-childness also cultivated a strong desire for connection. "Time alone" on your birthday didn't even compute in my brain … until she explained that she had recently been so busy with commitments that she just wanted a day, or part of a day, where she wasn't responsible for anybody or anything. Oh! That I could relate to. As you read earlier, I know a thing or two about wanting freedom from constriction. So we ended up enjoying quite a bit of time together on her birthday, but she also got in a sweet solo hike. Autonomy–connection. Openness–closedness. Intimacy … a paradoxical truth.

Relational tensions are managed best within safe relational spaces. A phrase I use frequently is, *create a space where if something good can happen, it will*.[13] That is what we do when we invite others to co-own private aspects of ourselves. Taking the risk to invite safe others to co-own aspects of our lives creates fertile spaces for intimacy to show up. This process of relational discovery is an essential element of intimacy, as you'll see in the next thread of this conversation.

---

13 Douglas L. Kelley, *Marital Communication* (Cambridge, England: Polity Press, 2012).

Thread 1.4

Intimacy as Discovery and Connection

A favorite childhood memory of mine is playing hide-and-seek. Perhaps you remember hiding, running to home base, and laughing with friends or parents. I recall playing in my front yard with neighborhood kids. There weren't very many places to hide—a few bushes, a low berm, and two palm trees. Just enough to conceal yourself until you had the chance to sprint to home base, your friend who was "it" in hot pursuit. However, as exciting as it was to find the ideal hiding place, the real exhilaration always came in being discovered.

Some of my best discovery memories are from a variation of hide-and-seek we played as a family when our oldest son, Jonathan, was three years old. At bedtime, Jonathan and I would go back to his bedroom and hide under his covers waiting for Ann ("Mom") to come in and find us. Over time we became more and more sophisticated, placing pillows in foot- and head-like lumps to throw Mom off the scent as we hid between the bed and the wall. The most striking part of this memory for me is when Ann would enter the room and Jonathan would become so excited at the prospect of being found that he would continually spew squeaks and giggles. "Shhhhh!" I would playfully exhort, "She's going to hear you." Ann knew better than to find us too quickly, which only added to the excitement. When she finally tossed off the blankets to discover us huddled together, Jonathan would laugh and squeal and there were hugs all around as we pulled her onto the bed. And, if I'm to be completely honest, I too felt the keen sense of anticipation not knowing exactly when we would be found!

We all have a deep desire to be discovered. Especially when that discovery brings connection by being fully accepted for who we are. I find it fascinating that various cultures throughout the world have their own versions of hide-and-seek, and there is even an international competition for adults that began in Italy in 2010. Discovery and connection appear to have universal appeal. So, let's take a closer look at how these elements work together to generate intimate space.

Common Perceptions

Intimacy is a word with which most of us are familiar, but seldom use. If I told my friend, Ron, "I'm feeling like we need to work on the intimacy in our relationship," Ron would definitely give me a strange look. However, I could safely say, "Dude, we've been too busy. We need to catch up."

Equally, it would seem odd to my wife's friend, Tami, if Ann said, "Tami, I feel like the intimacy in our relationship is waning." Instead, if she said, "Tami, I miss you. We need to spend some time together," Tami would most likely respond, "Let's get together!"

In my various research programs, I've found that many important relationship words, such as intimacy, love, and forgiveness, are used infrequently when people talk about their relationships. So in the *Intimacy in Personal Relationships (IPR)*[1] study I specifically asked people for their reflections on intimacy in all types of personal relationships—as friends, family, and lovers. Toward the beginning of the survey, while minds were fresh and uninfluenced by the bulk of the questionnaire, I asked participants to define intimacy. They provided a great variety of ideas. Some focused on closeness, connection, touching, sex, and affection. Others looked at understanding and vulnerability as you let someone into your inner circle of friends or family. Still others described intimacy as a desire, a craving, or an intellectual, emotional, or physical act.

My research team's analysis of this data determined that people see intimacy as a kind of behavior or experience or a combination of both. Intimate behavior has been described by researcher, Karen Prager, as including both nonverbal and verbal sharing (often described as self-disclosure by

---

1 See *Thread 3.1* for more detail on the study.

researchers). This was true for my *IPR* respondents, as well. Nonverbal expressions of intimacy were often described as a type of physicality, using terms such as touching, sex, hugging, and affection. And nonverbal displays of emotion were recognized as a powerful means of discovery and connection.

Growing Close 1.4.1

Interestingly, *IPR* respondents reported that intimacy could also be experienced through the absence of behavior, specifically, being silent with someone. I find silence particularly interesting when it is used to create intimate space. We tend to be primarily attuned to it (as we are with all communication behavior) when it shifts us from the norm ("Are you okay? You seem quiet today."). In this way, silence, when it fills space normally occupied by words, can be especially meaningful.

Silence is not limited to one particular relational meaning. Consider your own take on silence. Are you ever silent with your relationship partners? If so, what does your experience of silence reveal in these relationships? For instance, silence can come from having nothing to say or being preoccupied or fearful. *But intimate silence occurs when we feel comfortable and safe, aware of each other's presence.*

The firepit at our house is positioned so that Ann and I can watch the sunset on cool autumn days. Our senses reel in the refreshing breeze as the sun drops to the horizon. We've coined a phrase for these times—sundrops. Words can be interruptions during this time when a squeeze of the hand is all we need. Our sundrop moments illustrate another important aspect of silence—experiencing connection through presence and acceptance. What are your sundrop moments?

Words were equally important for *IPR* participants. When describing talk as a means of creating or demonstrating intimacy, they told us that intimate talk is an important means of giving people access to private information and feelings. And, as we discussed previously (see *Thread 1.3*), that when this access is given they begin to co-own this potentially intimate space.

Important to note is that verbal and nonverbal behaviors, in and of themselves, do not create an intimate moment. My *IPR* respondents were emphatic that it is the experience[2] of "intimate" behaviors that facilitates feeling emotionally connected or "close" to someone. In fact, close is the word that most completely represents how our respondents thought about intimacy, regardless of relationship type. And, our research participants went on to tell us that this sense of closeness was embedded in trusting someone with your vulnerability, and feeling comfortable and understood by your partner.

A Model of Intimate Relating (MIR)

The *IPR* study we've been discussing was designed around the *Access-Affect Model of Intimacy* that I formulated a decade ago.[3] This model was developed as a response to students and workshop participants who seemed to be relationally floundering, yearning for intimacy but confused as to how to make it happen. It also reflected my own desire to extend academic perspectives that had unanswered questions regarding the relationship between intimacy and love, especially within non-romantic relationships. As my thinking has continued to evolve, it's become clear that access and affect facilitate discovery and connection between relational partners, which in turn drives the intimacy experience.[4] As such, I have extended and renamed my former model as *A Model of Intimate Relating: The Process of Discovery and Connection*. Throughout our conversations, I refer to this model as *MIR* (*Model of Intimate Relating*).

---

2 Likewise, Prager argues that behaviors alone don't account for intimacy, but rather how individuals experience the behavior. For Prager, intimate experience includes affect (positive involvement, interest, and feelings regarding oneself, one's partner, or the interaction) and the perceptions of understanding one another. Karen J. Prager, *The Psychology of Intimacy* (New York: Guilford Press, 1995), 22.

3 Douglas L. Kelley, "Doing Meaningful Research: From No Duh to Aha! (A Personal Record)," *Journal of Family Communication* 8, no. 1 (2008): 1–18.

4 Just a note of reminder that I use partner to refer to anyone with whom we have a personal relationship (family, friend, lover).

Growing Close 1.4.2

Before we take a closer look at discovery and connection, consider these concepts in your own life. Are these new ideas for you or have you been aware of your desire to be discovered by and connected with others? What kinds of behaviors do you exhibit that indicate you are hoping for discovery and connection? How do your relational partners seek these elements in your relationships?

Here's one example of how Ann and I have worked out discovery and connection in our marriage. Ann's conflict style early in our marriage was retreat (in fairness, both of us preferred to runaway!). This approach to conflict made it difficult for me to *discover* what she was thinking and feeling. In fact, I misinterpreted her retreating behavior as indicating that she didn't want connection. I was so wrong. Actually, Ann retreated because she was afraid that the conflict would cause us to be *less* connected. Today, through a great deal of intentional work, we've both significantly improved at engaging conflict in ways that facilitate what we both really want—discovery and connection!

MIR takes the ideas of access and affect and refocuses them by using the terms *discovery* and *connection* to describe the key elements of intimacy. *Discovery* is based upon gaining access to one another, considering relationships to be much like the game hide-and-seek, as reflected upon at the beginning of this thread. Importantly, discovery emphasizes learning and understanding over simply gaining new information. Further, when intimate experience takes place, connection emerges out of discovery, emphasizing the feelings of closeness (positive affect) and perceived understanding that tie us together (see Table 1).[5]

---

5 Again, Karen Prager identifies intimate experience as positive feelings and perceived understanding. Karen J. Prager, *The Psychology of Intimacy* (New York: Guilford Press, 1995), 22.

TABLE 1 A Model of Intimate Relating (MIR): The Process of Discovery and Connection

Discovery through ...	Informational access
	Social access
	Physical access
	Psychological/emotional access
Connection through...	Feeling "close" (typically positive affect)
	Feeling understood and accepted

Discovery and Intimate Spaces

We begin our look at MIR with a focus on discovery. Think back to the previous conversational thread where we talked about privacy in terms of ownership and co-ownership. Let's expand that perspective. During my doctoral work I was fortunate to work with communication scholar, Judee Burgoon, on a research study that emphasized different aspects of the privacy process.[6] She based this work on Altman and Taylor's notion of access[7] and basically conceptualized privacy as the ability to restrict access.[8] From this perspective, privacy is freedom from unwanted intrusions of our informational space (past, present, future), physical space (touch, sight, sounds, smells, proximity), social space (when, how often, where, and with whom we interact), and psychological space (thoughts, attitudes, feelings).

I picked up on this perspective in a little article I wrote, "Privacy in Marital Relationships,"[9] that was read by at least three people (if you count me twice and my wife and my mom as half each, since they only read the first few pages). That article didn't change the world, but it did set me on a path that I'm still pursuing some 30 years later. It seemed to me that the flip side of privacy (restricting access), was intimacy (granting access). Choosing to let people into our private spaces, giving them access to ourselves as persons, allowing them to discover us, is central to what it means to be

6 Judee K. Burgoon et al., "Maintaining and Restoring Privacy Through Communication in Different Types of Relationships," *Journal of Social and Personal Relationships* 6, no. 2 (1989): 131–58, https://doi.org/10.1177/026540758900600201.

7 Irwin Altman, Anne Vinsel, and Barbara B. Brown, "Dialectic Conceptions in Social Psychology: An Application to Social Penetration and Privacy Regulation," *Advances in Experimental Social Psychology* 14 (1981): 107–60, https://doi.org/10.1016/S0065-2601(08)60371-8.

8 Judee K. Burgoon, "Privacy and Communication," in *Communication Yearbook* 6, ed. Michael Burgoon (Beverly Hills, CA: Routledge, 1982), 206–49.

9 Douglas L. Kelley, "Privacy in Marital Relationships," *Southern Speech Communication Journal* 53, no. 4 (1988): 441–56, https://doi.org/10.1080/10417948809372741.

Growing Close 1.4.3

A few years ago Ann and I were in the Paris airport trying to reschedule a flight that had been disrupted by a local airport strike. While standing in line with others, a middle-aged American male talked disparagingly about the French, their customs, and their language. He continually complained that the French didn't do things in the same ways as Americans. He had come to France to complete a job. Three months later, he left with little evidence of having interacted with the culture or having grown or learned. In that same line was a graduate student who had been living in France to learn the language and culture. I'm admittedly biased here, but it was refreshing to hear her stories of experiencing and learning to understand French culture. She spent her three months open, curious, and interested. The point is, that simply having access to something doesn't mean you discover it. Ann and I wouldn't choose to live exactly as the French live, but we did have a wonderful time discovering France during our time there.

Are there relationships in your life to which you have access, but have never chosen to discover the other person? As we've discussed, we make decisions about which relationships to grow deep and which to stabilize at less intimate levels. But, many of us have friendships, children and parents, or even romantic partners with whom we coexist. Is there someone in your life who is giving you access, that you could choose to discover?

intimate. This should sound familiar, because it is the basic idea behind Altman and Taylor's *social penetration theory* (aka, *onion skin theory*, that we discussed in *Thread 1.3* of this conversation).

Intimacy's relationship to access becomes most clear when considering intimacy violations. How do you feel when someone enters your personal space (the invisible bubble between you and others) without permission?

Or, when someone reads personal thoughts and feelings in a text, e-mail, or journal that was not intended for them to see? Or, when a good friend co-owns a secret of yours and shares that secret without your permission? Our responses to these violations suggest that they are more than just relational faux pas. We experience them as violations of our intimate space.[10]

So, access is the beginning point of discovery and may take place in any of the four privacy dimensions described by Burgoon (informational, social, physical, and psychological).[11] For our purposes, it will serve us well to flip these four privacy dimensions into what I call *intimate spaces*.[12] That is, when we gain access to one another's informational, social, physical, and psychological spaces we have the opportunity to discover one another, growing into greater intimacy.

Discovery of these intimate spaces involves more than simple access. The nature of discovery is to encounter something new, novel, unexpected. and to approach it with an attitude of learning and understanding. Certainly, we have all observed or experienced relationships where partners live or work in close proximity with one another, but experience little intimacy. Through lack of attention, empathy, or thoughtful consideration they simply coexist. In sharp contrast, discovery beckons us to explore, learn, understand. Like visiting a foreign country, we have the choice to engage the new culture (our relational partner) with curiosity and interest, as opposed to clinging to our own norms and understanding.

It can be helpful to think of our intimate spaces as living quarters—the deeply personal spaces where we live out our lives. These rooms and hidden passageways provide a picture of relational depth as we provide access to others within any given intimate space. My friend Michael, for example, took me down one of his secret passageways when he revealed that Michael wasn't the name he was born with. He invited me into an intimate space when he went on to explain, "I realize now that I changed my name to Michael when I was 13 because I so badly wanted my dad's respect and love (his dad was named Michael). I've decided it is time for me to have my own identity by returning to my given name–Ben." This was quite a shock, since his identity in my mind was "Michael." He didn't look like a "Ben" to me.

---

10 Note that the focus on intimacy as I am conceptualizing it includes discovery with feelings of connection. This excludes unwanted access, such as informational or physical privacy violations. Similarly, Prager focuses on positive experience.

11 Judee K. Burgoon, "Privacy and Communication," in *Communication Yearbook* 6, ed. Michael Burgoon (Beverly Hills, CA: Routledge, 1982), 206–49.

12 *Intimate spaces* can be micro (interactional elements between two people) or macro (the overall view of our relationship). It should be noted that Karen Prager (1995) also discusses intimacy as including both intimate interactions and intimate relationships.

But, more important was recognizing that he trusted me enough to take me into an intimate passageway that linked together his informational and psychological intimate spaces.

Viewing intimate spaces as the living quarters, let's look at the multiple rooms, secret passageways, and chambers of each of the four intimate spaces. Our informational intimate space includes everything from our names (posted on the door), to our financial debt (hidden in a desk drawer in the study), to all the quirky and embarrassing and even hurtful events we've experienced in our pasts (definitely kept in a secret chamber that few ever know about). As we saw in the previous example with Ben, letting others into our informational intimate space often lets them into other intimate spaces, as well. Consider how informing a romantic partner, "Let's just be friends," is much more than a relationship report. It suddenly opens the door to your psychological intimate space, as well.

The intimate space reserved for our social selves contains *who* gets time with us, *what* we talk about or do together, *how* we interact with one another, and *when* and *where* we interact with others. For instance, with a new friend or dating partner we often respond immediately to texts, are available at almost all hours of the day, discuss varied topics, include access to our private Instagram accounts, and communicate in a variety of ways like engaging in serious talk and playfulness. Ben's disclosure to me, that his birth name was not Michael, felt deep because he took time to tell me about it privately and our conversation ranged from deep talk about his dad to playful banter about the name change. If I had found out about the name change on Facebook, as one of his 641 friends, I wouldn't have had the same feeling of closeness that I experienced as we talked deeply and laughed late into the evening.

Physical intimate space includes touch but is comprised of anything related to our physical senses. Granting physical access to others includes a willingness to be seen (all families who share a common living space have a certain level of intimacy from simply observing one another), to be heard (I will take a difficult phone call from my mother, even while you are in the room), to be smelled (are you close enough friends to work out together?), to be tasted (mmm, is that strawberry lip gloss?) and, of course, all kinds of touch from utilitarian helping touch to affectionate touch. Returning to Ben's name revelation, besides giving me access to his informational and psychological intimate space, he let me into his physical intimate space by sharing with me face-to-face—the tone of his voice and facial expressions revealing parts of his story.

Psychological intimate space is where we store the private thoughts, feelings, attitudes, and values central to our self-identity. These aspects of our lives are often warehoused in secret passageways or behind locked doors in order to protect ourselves from rejection or misunderstanding. Because of this, it is common to find ourselves reticent to reveal our deepest hopes, dreams, and fears, even to a close partner or family member. Thankfully, however, our desire to be "discovered" by a relational partner in a way that is safe and connecting often warrants taking the risk of inviting others into our psychological intimate space. We see this when one partner first mumbles the words, "I love you," or when a young man has the "coming out" talk with his parents – both actions that invite significant risk of rejection, but equally create opportunity for a deeply intimate experience. For this reason, risking shared psychological intimate space is essential to developing our intimate relationships. Returning to Ben's name change, he and I remain close to this day because of his willingness to let me co-own part of his story regarding his identity and his complex relationship with his father.

Connection and Intimate Spaces

Discovery through access to our intimate spaces is clearly central to creating intimacy, but connection completes the intimacy experience. As our *IPR* survey respondents indicated, "feeling close" is strongly related to our sense of intimacy. It's not just someone gaining access into our intimate spaces, or us getting into theirs, it's what we feel when we're in there.

Think about purchasing a new home. You call your mortgage broker and in about three minutes she has detailed knowledge of your finances. "I see that you still owe money on your car and are still paying off your student loans. Oh, you like shopping at The Apothecary!" If you are like me, this process is a little unsettling. Although the broker has access to my private information, I don't feel an intimate connection with her.

Date rape provides a more poignant example of how intimacy is necessarily more than access. During this heinous personal violation, someone has had access to one's physical and psychological intimate spaces, resulting in great trauma and feelings related to disconnection, such as fear, contempt, or disgust. The paring of forced access and strong negative emotions is tragic in so many ways and highlights the normative expectation that *intimate experience includes a sense of feeling close, facilitated by the right to grant or deny access to our intimate spaces.*

In my original intimacy model, I identified the connection aspect of intimacy as affect—particularly, positive affect. And, although I still believe that to be true, the role of affect has become much more complex in my own mind.

One facet that adds complexity is that emotions are frequently experienced in clusters. For example, one study of relationship transgression, by Guerrero and Cole, found that offended parties may respond to relational offenses with a variety of emotions. In particular, relational partners experiencing fidelity violations, such as sexual infidelity or other third-party involvement, were likely to experience vulnerability, anger, embarrassment, and shock, whereas those experiencing honesty violations such as deception and misrepresentation of relational intent were prone to experience vulnerability, shock, and distress.

Guerrero and Cole's study focused on negative emotions, but equally conceivable, and even more complex, is when transgressions trigger emotional clusters containing both positive and negative emotions. Guerrero states as much when she concludes that individuals in conflict may feel competing impulses, such as wanting to disconnect from a hurtful partner and, yet, somehow stay close.[13] Consider how betrayal might trigger anger while also eliciting awareness of the love you have for your offending partner. Human relationships are most certainly complex.

A second facet that complicates the connection/affect aspect of intimacy involves the distinct difference between experiencing soft emotions (sadness, hurt) and hard emotions (rage, bitterness). Both soft and hard emotions are considered "negative" in the sense that they are precipitated by negative events and don't feel "good." However, at times we may desire, even embrace, these emotions in ways that are productive for ourselves and our relationships. Perhaps this is most evident with the soft emotion, sadness. Of course, we don't want things to happen that make us sad, but sadness itself is a beautiful emotion that often accompanies the experience of loss—loss of someone or something we love or deeply value. Interestingly, one of my graduate students, Angela, who did some editing for me on this project, made the following comment after she read this section:

> *For me personally, I think sadness can sometimes even be something that is emotionally cleansing. I love to watch* Grey's Anatomy *and I cry a lot when I do, and afterwards I just feel so much better because in a weird kind of way it feels like I had the opportunity to release, express and feel the sadness that I've felt about things in my own life that I never really got to express because of social constraints, responsibilities and just because life gets 'in the way.'*

---

13   Laura K. Guerrero, "Emotion and Communication in Conflict Interaction," In *The SAGE Handbook of Conflict Communication*, eds. John G. Oetzel and Stella Ting-Toomey (Thousand Oaks, CA: SAGE, 2013), 105–32.

Angela's words beautifully reflect the value in experiencing "negative" emotions. Yet, experiencing positive aspects of negative affect is not limited to soft emotions. For instance, marriage researchers are finding that the hard emotion, anger, is not necessarily as damaging as once thought. Anger is an engaging emotion that, when expressed appropriately, can evidence the emotional connection still present between two relational partners.

So, *MIR*,[14] recognizes the complexity of human emotional response and, rather than focusing on positive affect, emphasizes emotions and feelings of closeness. We previously discussed in *Thread 1.2* that a primary reason we seek positive affect is the connection it signals between us and the world in which we live. As psychologist, Karen Prager, suggests, intimate interactions are typically accompanied by warm feelings that lead to an enduring sense of affection, over time.[15] And, yet, certain "negative" emotional experiences may also signal closeness in a relationship. Especially, when those experiences are shared and trigger the perception that one is understood and accepted or demonstrate that one's partner is still invested in the relationship.[16]

Ultimately it is the dynamic relationship between discovery and connection that counts. Let's look at Ramon and Regina's troubled marriage as an example of the complex relationship between discovery within various intimate spaces and connection. Figure 1.4.1. shows how connection and discovery within each of Ramon and Regina's intimate spaces shifted from early marriage to the dissolution of the marriage. Notice that while certain aspects of intimacy diminished over time, other aspects held steady or even increased. Ramon and Regina's informational discovery actually increased a small amount after their divorce because during conflict new information surfaced. Likewise, psychological access increased during the divorce process because they were more assertive and honest with each other about how they felt during their marriage and, at times, more vulnerable during conflict. This all led to greater discovery, but not necessarily greater connection. And, as you would presume, after the divorce their physical and social access to one another diminished significantly, although,

---

14 My renamed model, *Model of Intimate Relating*

15 Karen J. Prager, *The Psychology of Intimacy* (New York: Guilford Press, 1995).

16 To be clear, the closeness experienced with certain emotions such as sadness and anger, should not be confused with increases in negative behaviors or reductions of positive behaviors. Research consistently demonstrates, that less positivity and humor and laughter, and more negativity and reciprocated negativity are related to lower levels of relationship satisfaction. Douglas L. Kelley, *Marital Communication*, (Cambridge, England: Polity Press, 2012); Valerie Manusov, "Reacting to Changes in Nonverbal Behaviors Relational Satisfaction and Adaptation Patterns in Romantic Dyads," *Human Communication Research* 21, no. 4 (1995): 456–477, https://doi.org/10.1111/j.1468-2958.1995.tb00354.x.

FIGURE 1.4.1 Ramon and Regina's Discovery and Connection over Time*

Informational	low ....EM*......AD............high
Social	low ......................AD..EM.......high
Physical	low .........AD..EM....high
Psychological	low ....EM............AD...............high
Connection	low .......................AD...EM..........high

*EM = early marriage; AD = after divorce.

because they have young children, social access continued through social media (sharing pictures of the kids' events) and dropping the kids off at one another's homes.

Mutual Discovery and Connection

Consider a final perspective as we wrap up this thread of the conversation. Implicit in our discussion up to this point is that giving others access to our intimate spaces, and being willing to accept invitations into others' personal spaces, provides a means of mutual discovery and connection.

Note the emphasis on *mutual* discovery and connection. Intimacy requires the involvement of both parties. It is reciprocal. This distinguishes personal intimate relationships from professional relationships that involve unilateral (one-sided) access and discovery. For example, relationships with therapists and doctors require clients and patients to provide certain types of access (generally informational, physical, or psychological). This access is typically unilateral, one person being discovered while the other stays hidden within her or his professional roles (although a doctor or therapist may strategically choose to share personal information). You might feel something of intimacy, even if you are the only one giving access, but the relationship is limited unless discovery and feelings of connection are mutual.

This same process can be true, even in our friendships and romantic relationships. When one partner stays hidden in his or her role as friend or sexual partner and, as such, discovery and connection remain minimal or one-sided, the process of intimacy is stunted. As the old saying goes, *it takes two to tango*. It's not "wrong" when relationships develop unilaterally. Actually, it is quite common. However, it is important to be aware that, like putting a governor on a car to restrict its speed, intimacy is limited when discovery and connection are not mutual.

Growing Close 1.4.4

Take a minute to consider how mutuality, or its lack, is evident in your own relational experience. Some of our relationships feel more personal than others. They consist of more mutual sharing, access, vulnerability. More shared discovery. How has a sense of mutual discovery affected your personal connections with others?

Among my friends, there is one, Robin, who is pretty much an open book. When we grab dinner together he is immediately forthcoming about what's going on in his life and how it affects him. I'm pretty good at this, too. Of course, we also talk about the U.S. Open and Robin's homemade brew! Neither of us dominates. It is an equal time of discovering one another as friends. Another friend, Jack, is much more cautious and analytic. He is a valuable source of insight when things are tough in my life and loads of fun, however, I typically don't feel as close to Jack as I do to Robin since Jack doesn't reciprocate my self-revelations. One exception to this occurred during a year when Jack was going through some pretty heavy issues. Out of his own con-fusion and loss he finally opened up and I felt renewed possibilities in our friendship. However, much to my disappointment, once his problems leveled out, he went back into reserved, con-trolled, analytic mode. He is still a valued friend, I just don't feel as close or safe in our relationship as I did when he was most vulnerable.

Intimate Reflections

Opening ourselves to discovery and connection is exhilarating and beautiful when it works. There is an exquisite joy experienced when we join in relationship hide-and-seek and are "found" by the significant others in our lives. This relational unearthing is driven by many things, one of which is curiosity. In the following thread, I explore the benefits of cultivating a relationally curious mind, chief of which is to discover and connect more deeply with others and ourselves.

But, of course, discovery and connection are risky business. When we give others access to our intimate spaces and allow ourselves to feel positive emotions for them, we become vulnerable. Once I've been discovered, I am vulnerable to being hurt by you—intentionally or not. And, once I've experienced positive connection with you, I'm vulnerable to losing our valued relationship—intentionally or not. So, hang on, because the next couple of threads look at curiosity and vulnerability and the ways both can ultimately enrich our lives.

Thread 1.5

Curiosity: The Discovery of Self and Other

As a social scientist, discovery is what I do—discovering new information, discovering new ways of connecting ideas, discovering novel approaches to doing relationships. Key to this approach to career and life is *curiosity*—pondering, wondering, tinkering. Based on what we have just discussed in the two previous threads of our conversation, I believe that adopting a *curious* approach to life can change the way we experience relationships and greatly enhance our experience of intimacy.

Elizabeth Gilbert, best known for her travel and spiritual autobiography, *Eat, Pray, Love,* writes about curiosity in, *Big Magic.*[1] Here, she encourages readers to have the courage to go where their curiosity takes them. As long as that curiosity is leading you into healthy spaces, for you and your relational partners, that sounds like good advice.

In a recent podcast exploring curiosity, Gilbert makes an interesting distinction between pursuing curiosity and pursuing your "passion." She argues that telling people to pursue their passion can at times be damaging. I agree. *Pursuing your passion* is an American discourse that suggests each person must find his or her unique role in life in order

---

1 Elizabeth Gilbert, *Big Magic: Creative Living Beyond Fear* (New York: Riverhead Books, 2015).

to have value. A useful perspective for many of us. However, this discourse may also subtly communicate that you are most valuable when you exhibit individual achievement and that there is something wrong with you if you fail to identify your passion and pursue it "passionately." In this way, the push to "pursue your passion" can result in shame for those who don't know what their passion is, don't want to know what it is, don't think they have the means to pursue it, or simply view life from a different cultural vantage point.

Take a moment to meet my friend, Amy. Amy works with college students and, for years, has told me that each day she wakes up thinking, "God has me here to unlock the potential of this generation of students." Wow! Impressive. I kind of wish I had that. However, I just don't experience life that way.

I work with college students, too. I also hope to unlock their potential. However, my "passion of the day" is largely a result of where my curiosity leads. In the classroom, or a community workshop, that may mean tossing out a few ideas (related to course content, of course) and seeing where our conversation takes us. In my research it often means asking questions and then examining participants' responses with a sense of openness to discover what new ideas and perspectives are waiting to be uncovered (that characterizes much of the IPR study referenced in previous threads). In fact, a couple of hours from now my research team and I will look at IPR participant responses (reported in *Conversation Three*) to the question, "How has forgiveness created or exhibited intimacy in your relationships?" These sessions are marvelous times of discovery as I listen to my graduate students engage the rich perspectives offered by our respondents.

Though we may have personal preferences for one or the other, both curiosity and passion can be valued aspects of our lives and relationships. However, of the two, I think curiosity has largely been underappreciated when it comes to relating with others.

Curiosity has the potential to transform the ways we approach our relationship partners. Taking a curious approach to relationships suggests discovering our relational partners, rather than simply using them to fulfill our wants and desires. This perspective shift avoids framing our relationships as possessions primarily valued for getting our own needs met. Putting curiosity at our relational core provides a means of viewing personal relationships as spaces given to exploration, learning, and understanding. The upshot is that approaching our relationships with curiosity encourages discovery through our conversations and conflicts, play and grief, sex and forgiveness.

Famed anthropologist, Ashley Montagu, considers curiosity a neotenous trait, a youthful quality essential to healthy development and survival.[2] Neoteny is a process whereby individuals carry juvenile characteristics into adulthood. According to Montagu, maintaining "young" characteristics, such as creativity, play, flexibility, work, and, of course, curiosity is critical for healthy maturation and aging. From this perspective, curiosity is considered an essential element of our humanness. And, as we will examine more closely in the next thread, it is an essential characteristic of intimacy that prevents vulnerability from turning into selfishness.[3]

When nurtured and cultivated, curiosity leads us to awareness and, ultimately, discovery. When we are curious, we attend to the world with a sense of openness and the hope of receiving. We are alert, outward focused, interested in discovering why and how things work, as opposed to maintaining a narcissistic relationship frame where we are intent on telling others what we already "know." This curious relationship framework creates relational spaces where good things can happen, most often developing a sense of closeness with those we are discovering.[4]

Intimate Reflections

One of the marvelous things about curiously discovering others is that, when attentive, we discover ourselves as well. Self-focused responses that assert our own experiences and defend our own positions teach us very little about ourselves. However, when we listen to and observe our partners' thoughts, desires, and emotional responses, we have the opportunity to discover more about our own. *In discovering you, I discover me.* Or, as Desmond Tutu puts it when describing *Ubuntu*, "A person is a person through other persons."[5]

Still, for many of us, it is a fear of self-discovery and potential vulnerability that keeps us from curiosity, discovery of others, and connection. In fact,

---

2 Montagu, Ashley. *Growing Young.* 2nd ed. (Westport, CT: Bergin & Garvey, 1989).

3 Julia C. Obert, "What We Talk About When We Talk About Intimacy," *Emotion, Space, and Society* 21 (2016): 25–32.

4 Todd B. Kashdan et al., "When Curiosity Breeds Intimacy: Taking Advantage of Intimacy Opportunities and Transforming Boring Conversations," *Journal of Personality* 79, no. 6 (2011): 1067–99, doi:10.1111/j.1467-6494.2010.00697.x; Todd B. Kashdan and John E. Roberts, "Trait and State Curiosity in the Genesis of Intimacy: Differentiation From Related Constructs," *Journal of Social and Clinical Psychology* 23, no. 6 (2004): 792–816, doi:10.1521/jscp.23.6.792.54800.

5 *Ubuntu* is discussed more fully in *Thread 1.4.* Desmond Tutu, *No Future Without Forgiveness* (New York, NY: Doubleday, 1999), 31.

Growing Close 1.5.1

**A Curiosity-based Approach to
Discovery in Relationships**

The following examples contrast curious responses that lead to discovery and connection with
retorts that simply assert our own experience or
positions. Take time at the end of each conversation to imagine potentially different outcomes
between self-focused and curiosity-based responses.

Conversation One: Self-focused approach

Friend: I'm thinking about heading to Seattle this summer.

You: I lived in Seattle for three years and couldn't handle the rain.

*Write out how you think this conversation might
continue:*

_____

Conversation One: Curiosity-based approach

Friend: I'm thinking about heading to Seattle this summer.

You: Really? What's attracting you to Seattle?

*Write out how you think this conversation might
continue:*

_____

Conversation Two: Self-focused approach

Your partner: I think the guest bath would look good in gray.

You: Gray will be too dark. We should do white to lighten the space.

Write out how you think this conversation might continue:

_____

Conversation Two: Curiosity-based approach

Friend: I think the guest bath would look good in gray.

You: What do you think gray will bring to our small guest bath?

Write out how you think this conversation might continue:

_____

Conversation Three: Self-focused approach

Friend: I'm not sure what do about my relationship with Pat..

You: In my experience, long-distance relationships never work.

Write out how you think this conversation might continue.

_____

Conversation Three: Curiosity-based approach

Your partner: I'm not sure what do about my relationship with Pat.

You: Tell me more about what's going on between you and Pat.

Write out how you think this conversation might continue.

_____

many of us use self-focused communication to maintain a sense of control (If I keep talking or assert my position I remove some of the unpredictability of the conversation.). This false sense of certainty may lead us to avoid the uncertainty and vulnerability that naturally accompany curiosity and, of course, intimacy. Our next conversational thread tackles this very conundrum—if vulnerability is necessary for intimacy, how do we experience it in ways that are safe and promote closeness?

The Problem with Intimacy

Vulnerability

My wife, Ann, and I were working at a youth camp during our first year of marriage. I had a position on staff, but Ann was along for the ride hoping to find connection and purpose wherever she could. The first few days were pretty lonely for her. Then, one morning, over coffee, she ended up in a revealing conversation with Miriam, another staff member. Although they didn't know each other well, Miriam began to share about her childhood abuse and how lingering effects from this experience were affecting her marriage. Ann listened intently and, then, as they parted to take care of the day's tasks, gave her a big hug. Later that day, she excitedly told me about her conversation with Miriam. This new friendship seemed the answer to her loneliness. Possibly, this was her purpose for being at camp. That evening at dinner, however, when Ann waved across the dining commons to Miriam, Miriam only gave a brief wave and went on her way. The next morning when Ann ran into her at the coffee shop, Miriam was pleasant, but disengaged. After a week of this behavior, Ann asked Miriam if they could talk. "Sure," Miriam quickly responded, "as soon as I can find some time." That time never came.

Vulnerability. Essential to intimacy. Yet, often accompanied by strong feelings of risk and fear that undermine the very intimacy we all seek.

Fear and Risk

Relational risk is hard. Think back to the essential relationship paradox we discussed in *Thread 1.3—intimacy emerges as autonomous partners struggle to connect*. In tension with the very connection we all want is the risk of losing the autonomy we cherish. So how do we respond to the risk inherent in this relational tension? One study focusing on the relationship between connectedness and self-protection found that people lower in self-esteem engaged in more self-protection as they simultaneously sought connection. On the other hand, people higher in self-esteem were able to tolerate the risk that comes with depending on others in order to connect. In the previous example with Miriam and Ann, both wanted connection, but after sharing so vulnerably with someone she didn't know well, Miriam's fear overrode her desire to deepen the relationship. Perhaps, low self-esteem caused her self-protection goals to kick in, thwarting the very connection for which she hoped.

Miriam's story showcases fear as a common emotional reaction when we open ourselves to others. Inherent to giving relational partners access to our intimate spaces is the fear of that access being used to hurt us (intentionally or not). This is why those with whom we are closest are able to hurt us most deeply. Revelation of a personal secret, past hurts surfacing during a conflict, and unmet expectations all hurt more when coming from a close friend, a romantic partner, or a family member whom we have trusted. Yet, paradoxically, living with this risk in an emotionally safe relationship stimulates the development of deep intimacy as it reveals trust and an expectation for empathy and compassion. Vulnerability is certainly the hallmark of intimacy.[1]

Three Intimacy-Reducing Reactions to Vulnerability

Vulnerability doesn't guarantee intimacy. Fear of vulnerability and its inherent risks often trigger one of three reactions that actually shut down intimacy: restrict access, control the environment, and shut off the inner self.

When we *restrict access*, we prevent others from gaining entrance into our intimate spaces.[2] We live in such a way that our relational partners never really get to know us. For instance, when I restrict information you have

---

1 Douglas L. Kelley, *Just Relationships: Living Out Social Justice as Mentor, Family, Friend, and Lover* (New York: Routledge, 2017).

2 It should be noted that there are times when restricting access is an appropriate means of setting boundaries in unhealthy relationships.

about me by limiting talk, social interaction, and the opportunity to observe my life (e.g., I might choose to work alone and live alone), I limit your ability to hurt me psychologically and emotionally.

We often try to *control the environment* when we are in situations where we can't restrict the access people have to us. In this case, we hope to limit negative effects by holding rigidly to self-protective rules and norms. Unfortunately, this approach often ends up creating distance between relational partners since formal structures tend to keep us stuck in prescribed roles ("Children don't question their mothers!" "Real men don't show their emotions to other men.") rather than engaging in more personal communication.

Finally, when we seem unable to control our vulnerability by restricting access or controlling the environment, we may choose to emotionally *shut off our inner self* in order to manage potential pain—essentially, "If I can't feel anything, you can't hurt me." For example, the process of emotional numbing is a common response from those who have experienced past abuse. One day a neighbor of mine, Stan, walked across the street while I was trimming trees in our front yard. He and his wife, Sandy, had divorced a few years back and he was now in a serious relationship with another woman. He knew I taught about relationships and volunteered, "You know, I was abused as a child. To cope, I shut off all of my emotions. It was all I could do to survive. Through counseling I learned that my 'emotion switch' had stayed off during my marriage with Sandy. I was a good guy, but Sandy couldn't ever really connect to me because I was emotionally numb. I guess it was just too scary for me. It's too bad I didn't realize this before we divorced, but she's happy now, and I'm finally in a healthy relationship."

Each of these three approaches to managing vulnerability is based on decisions to be unavailable to others. And, while they may be effective to some extent in the short run, they run the risk of damaging our ability to experience intimacy over time. So how do we cultivate relational spaces where we can be genuinely and safely vulnerable with others? Following we look at three concepts central to experiencing vulnerability in a healthy manner: trust, courage, and curiosity. And, in the next thread we explore the possibility that *full love* creates a safe space for intimacy.

Trust

I'm writing this portion of the book at a family camp,[3] on a lake in the Adirondack Mountains of New York that has been in my wife's family since it was built by her great, great grandfather in 1891. A highlight of this trip has been the week-long visit of my oldest son, Jon, his wife, Emily, and my three grandchildren. A few days into their stay we were all out at the swimming dock. Two-and-a-half-year-old Atticus had been jumping off the dock to Jon's waiting hands as Jon tread water. This time, however, Jon was on the dock with Atticus and I was treading water, so Jon encouraged Atti to jump to me. Atti and I have a good relationship, but I'm not his dad and we live in different cities so we've had limited time together. I knew full well that he might only feel safe jumping to "Daddy," so I was prepared not to take it too personally if he said "NO WAY!" That said, he hesitated only a fraction of a second and then launched his body into the air toward my outstretched arms. I was in the club! Trust.

Trust has been of keen interest to researchers examining relationship reconciliation (and potential restoration of intimacy).[4] After experiencing a relational transgression, a central challenge is to re-establish damaged trust.[5] One way to think about trust is to consider whether one's relational partner can be "counted on."[6] In particular, can I count on you to be a "safe" person for me, physically, emotionally, psychologically? Translated, that could mean, *can I trust you not to intentionally hurt me? To be available and respond kindly and helpfully when I need it? To be committed to me and our relationship?*

There are two primary ways of rebuilding trust in our relationships: words and consistent action over time.

Beginning with words, I've come to very much appreciate the ideas of apology and promise. If I have betrayed your trust, you might expect at the very least that I say, "I'm sorry." In a recent book on conflict, forgiveness, and reconciliation, colleagues and I suggest that *full apology* can be quite powerful in restoring safety and trust in a relationship:

---

3 In the Adirondack Mountains, cabins are referred to as camps.

4 Everett L. Worthington, Jr., *Forgiveness and Reconciliation: Theory and Application* (New York: Routledge, 2006).

5 Douglas L. Kelley, Vincent R. Waldron, and Dayna N. Kloeber, *A Communicative Approach to Conflict, Forgiveness, and Reconciliation: Reimagining Our Relationships* (New York: Routledge, 2019).

6 Caryl E. Rusbult et al. "Forgiveness and Relational Repair," in *Handbook of Forgiveness*, ed. Everett L. Worthington, Jr. (New York: Routledge, 2005), 185–205.

[T]he humility necessary to offer a sincere apology helps to restore a sense of equity in the relationship, and an apology that demonstrates true understanding, remorse, and a commitment to change future behavior helps the offended party feel safe, and that the hurtful behavior is less likely to occur again.[7]

As noted in the preceding quote, an important aspect of apology is promise—committing to a positive relational future. Philosopher, Hannah Arendt, tells us, "The remedy for unpredictability, for the chaotic uncertainty of the future, is contained in the faculty to make and keep promises." To make a promise is, essentially, to commit verbally to a given course of action ("I promise to work on my tone of voice," "I promise I will focus on listening more attentively."). Researchers have found that when promises offer a trustworthy, intentional look at the future, along with interpersonal

Growing Close 1.6.1

In the forgiveness and reconciliation research that Vince Waldron and I have conducted, we've noticed that apologies often include promise, such as, "I'll never do it again!" Yet, psychologists Everett Worthington and Dewitt Drinkard suggest that this kind of promise, while understandable, is unrealistic.[12] They suggest that it is much more useful to realize change takes time and, as humans, we are going to make mistakes. This returns us to the idea of paradox that we discussed in *Thread 1.3*. When I promise, I must somehow recognize my imperfection, but also help you feel assured that my honest intent is to change, over time ... and that I'm worth the risk!

Promises aren't limited to "fixing" transgressions. They can also be used to set up guidelines so

7   Douglas L. Kelley, Vincent R. Waldron, and Dayna N. Kloeber, *A Communicative Approach to Conflict, Forgiveness, and Reconciliation: Reimagining Our Relationships* (New York: Routledge, 2019), 119.

that, hopefully, transgressions don't happen. Traditional wedding vows, for example, are built around promise: "I, _____, take you, _____, to be my wife/husband, and these things I promise you: I will be faithful to you and honest with you; I will respect, trust, help, and care for you; I will share my life with you; I will forgive you as we have been forgiven; and I will try with you better to understand ourselves, the world and God; through the best and worst of what is to come, and as long as we live."[13]

Think back to a time when you made a promise to someone else, or they promised you. It may have been after a wrong done or in anticipation of a joint future together. What made the promise useful or not useful? Believable or not believable? Effective or not effective? How would you teach some to make a promise in such a way that it builds trust?

sensitivity, they help partners feel like justice (fairness) is being restored to the relationship.[8]

But words alone are insufficient to restore trust. One study with young children puts this in perspective. Researchers found that children as young as three years of age recognize how a promise is supposed to "work"— you do what you say you will do.[9] To maintain trust, promise must be followed by consistent action over time. Arendt's remedy for unpredictability, is not to simply make promises, but to *keep* them. Without promises we don't know if actions are intended to continue over the long haul. And, likewise, promises, without subsequent action, become hollow and empty.

---

8 Edward C. Tomlinson, "The Impact of Apologies and Promises on Post-Violation Trust: The Mediating Role of Interactional Justice," *The International Journal of Conflict Management* 23, no. 3 (2012): 224–47, 10.1108/10444061211248930.

9 Patricia Kanngiesser, Bahar Köymen, and Michael Tomasello, "Young Children Mostly Keep, and Expect Others to Keep, Their Promises," Journal of Experimental Child Psychology 159 (2017): 140–58, http://dx.doi.org/10.1016/j.jecp.2017.02.004.

10 Lutheran Wedding Vows, The Knot, "Traditional Wedding Vows From Various Religions," Theknot.com, June 07, 2019, accessed June 24, 2019, https://www.theknot.com/content/traditional-wedding-vows-from-various-religions.

Courage

One evening I sat alone by our fireplace contemplating Ann's and my marriage. We were in counseling and I was feeling a bit lost. I suddenly remembered that a couple months before our counselor had given me a link to a TEDx talk she thought I could use in one of my classes. It was Brené Brown's talk on vulnerability. One of the striking aspects of this talk is that Brené connects vulnerability to courage. After listening to her message I walked outside by our pool and gazed into the cosmos. Then, it was as if I heard the words, "You know the freedom you are looking for? This is the answer. You'll never be free unless you have the courage to be vulnerable."

Let's look more closely at how social work professor Brené Brown talks of courage and vulnerability. At this writing, her TEDx talk on vulnerability has received over 35 million views and been translated into 52 languages.[11] In her professional yet personal style, Professor Brown relays her research discoveries—vulnerability is essential for connection, and courage is essential to embrace vulnerability in a way that fosters intimacy. Rather than relying on withdrawal, control, or shutting down emotionally to protect ourselves (as previously discussed), Brown's research demonstrates that "whole hearted" people, those who live out of their authentic self, have the courage to be vulnerable in their personal relationships and "the willingness to do something with no guarantees." Listen in, to Brown's insights:

> *Courage, the original definition of courage, when it first came into the English language—it's from the Latin word "cor," meaning "heart"—and the original definition was to tell the story of who you are with your whole heart. And so these [whole-hearted] folks had, very simply, the courage to be imperfect. They had the compassion to be kind to themselves first and then to others, because, as it turns out, we can't practice compassion with other people if we can't treat ourselves kindly. And the last was they had connection, and—this was the hard part—as a result of authenticity, they were willing to let go of who they thought they should be in order to be who they were, which you have to absolutely do that for connection.*

As we just discussed in *Thread 1.5*, intimacy is partly about discovery of self and, as Brown exhorts us, partly about accepting our imperfections and treating ourselves kindly. This breeds a new kind of courage—even though you can still hurt me in my vulnerability, the hurt has limited effect

---

11   Brené Brown, "The Power of Vulnerability," filmed June 2010 at TEDxHouston, Houston, TX, video, https://www.ted.com/talks/brene_brown_on_vulnerability#t-12244.

because I have already accepted my imperfections. I have already chosen to treat myself well.

However, not to be missed is that connection is a result of an authenticity that goes beyond accepting imperfections, it embraces what we could call "true self." Brown's words, "they were willing to let go of who they thought they should be in order to be who they were, which you have to absolutely do that for connection," speak to a profound exercise of relational courage—we must learn to accept who we are, within the context of our relationships.

Growing Close 1.6.2

How might accepting your true self affect your relationships? What would it mean to even accept your imperfections? Not excuse the imperfections we all carry with us, but accept who you are and the fact that you aren't perfect. That you are unique and that you make mistakes. Are you able to embrace Thich Nhat Han's admonition to treat yourself with tenderness? If so, you would be freed from having to protect yourself through withdrawal, control, or emotional shutdown. How might this make you a more available (accessible) partner in your personal relationships

---

Indeed, Julien Mirivel describes this type of courage as a virtue of interpersonal communication. He emphasizes that courage isn't an absence of fear, but rather the willingness to act in spite of one's fear. Mirivel uses "coming out" stories as courage exemplars. Here gay individuals want to be honest with family and friends to build connection, but fear that their honesty will result in rejection. As we've discussed regarding relational paradox, struggles such as these can result in deep intimacy, but clearly they also run the risk of heartbreak and rejection. As such, we begin with the courageous act of accepting who we are, then courageously express our "true self" to those for whom we care.

Curiosity

In the previous thread, we discussed the importance of cultivating curiosity to more fully discover our partners and our own self. Curiosity creates an open, outward orientation toward life. English professor, Julia Obert, highlights curiosity in a thought-provoking theory of intimacy built around feeling-states that push and pull against one another to create a system of relationship checks and balances. These feeling-states consist of curiosity, vulnerability, empathy, and irreducibility (recognition that the "other" can never be completely known). In essence, she suggests that a compassionate, empathetic curiosity is necessary to engage one's own vulnerability and the vulnerability of others. Obert states that "curiosity without empathy can become aggression, vulnerability without curiosity can become selfishness." Interestingly, when all four elements are present, they create another inter-personal virtue, generosity. According to Obert, curiosity, vulnerability, and empathy are all open, generous orientations toward one's partner that, reciprocally, create an intimate space for the partner to be generous in return. And, may I suggest, that cultivating an open, generous orientation toward oneself is equally important in creating a healthy foundation for intimacy.

Intimate Reflections

In this conversational thread we have explored the challenging topic of vulnerability and the need for trust and courage to create a space for intimacy to happen. In particular, we have pondered the power and beauty of promise, and the foundation of empathic curiosity. But, still I hear my students' voices, "I like what you're suggesting here. I resonate with it. I even think it's beautiful in its own way. But ... *I keep getting hurt!*" In the words of a rather humorous country song:

> *You done stomped on my heart, and you mashed that sucker flat. You just sorta, stomped on my aorta!*[12]

How do we safeguard ourselves from "giving our heart away" and then getting crushed? I think part of the answer is *full love*. The next thread explores the idea of how a full conceptualization of love is our best chance at creating meaningful, rich, and safe intimate spaces.

---

12 Mason Williams, *You Done Stomped on My Heart* (New York: RCA Records, 1969), performed by John Denver.

Thread 1.7

Full Love

A Safe Space for Intimacy

Admittedly, I am a dog person. I truly love these personable companions. Last summer as we hiked the sacred mounds of the Hill of Tara in Ireland, an Irish Setter pup spotted me and with unbridled delight ran in my direction through the tall grass. I knelt down and he, with tail swishing and ears flying, lodged himself into my arms, becoming suddenly still as I scratched his head and ears. It just doesn't get much better than that.

One of the interesting things about dogs, is that they will look you straight in your eyes. This can be a form of aggression, but it is also a way to connect.[1] One of the reasons our family fell in love with our beagle/lab mix, Allen, was his use of eye contact. Many a morning, Ann and I will sit on a couch poolside at our home. This was one of Allen's favorite intimate spaces as he would hop up on the couch, lay his 60-pound frame across Ann's lap, and let her scratch his butt, back, and belly. If she stopped scratching, even for a moment, he would stretch upward until his long snout almost touched her nose, looking straight into her eyes as if to say, "You can't be serious!"

---

1 Alexandra Horowitz, *Inside of a Dog: What Dogs See, Smell, and Know* (New York: Scribner, 2009).

He also had an uncanny sense of interaction dynamics, placing himself between the standing legs of anyone whose voice sounded angry, harsh, or shrill. I remember standing during a rather heated discussion when the tone of my voice rose and I soon felt Allen wriggling his way between my legs, as if to say, "Chill out." He was also a bit of a worrier. When concerned about me, like when I was lying on the floor panting after a workout, he would come sniff through my hair, give me one lick in the face, and then lie down near me just for assurance.

Allen was a natural lover. I, on the other hand, have had a few things to learn from my wet-nosed friend. It's not that I didn't have love modelled to me as a child. Just the opposite. I was an only child and very close to both parents during my early years. After my parents' divorce my mom and I grew even closer, and my relationship with my dad was cemented by the close bond we had experienced when we lived at home together.

Yet, I learned that people loving people is complicated. The different ways that I experienced love with each parent taught me early on that love doesn't look the same across our varied relationships. Marriage, parenting, and friendship have all confirmed that to be true. And, for me, my parents' words when they were separating, "We love each, we just can't live together," sum up my need to better understand what love is.

In the IPR[2] study I've referenced throughout this conversation, I not only asked people about intimacy, I also prompted them to reflect on the nature of love. Across 197 responses we found a number of consistent themes. In particular, people wrote about caring and understanding. They also associated love with being happy. Loving relationships were described as safe places where you trust and are connected with others and can be yourself. Some of these themes should sound familiar from the previous threads of this conversation. They reflect the messy entanglement of people's understandings of love and intimacy. As this conversational thread unfolds, I will consider a number of different perspectives on love and then offer my own *Model of Full Love* to help untangle the love and intimacy conundrum. Let's begin by looking at some of the ways researchers have conceptualized love in personal relationships.

---

2 *Intimacy in Personal Relationships*

Social Science Perspectives on Love

In the early days of my academic career, I found it interesting that social scientists studying relationships gave relatively little attention to love. In my own field of communication, social scientific discussions of love were virtually non-existent until the last couple decades. In psychology, Susan and Clyde Hendricks[3] carried the torch early on, and Robert Sternberg's Triangular Theory of Love became an oft-cited perspective.[4] Sternberg's theory had a significant influence on my own thinking, as well.

For Sternberg, three components determine the way love is experienced: intimacy, passion, and decision/commitment. For example, romantic love is comprised of intimacy and passion, paralleled by companionate love which is characterized by intimacy and decision/commitment. Infatuation, as you would guess, is simply passion without intimacy or commitment, whereas consummate love encompasses all three of the love components. Sternberg's model is intuitively appealing in that it provides a way to understand a wide variety of love experiences.

More recently Barbara Fredrickson has taken an emotion-based approach to understanding the nature of love. Fredrickson provides fresh insights, going so far as to state, "Love blossoms virtually anytime two or more people—even strangers—connect over a shared positive emotion, be it mild or strong."[5] The blossoming of love can be understood as *positivity resonance* between people. Think of positivity resonance as relational partners mirroring a trio of experiences between each other. This occurs when loving partners mirror the positivity in one another's emotional states, fall into biobehavioral synchrony through mirroring each other's gestures and even biochemistry (for example, synchrony in levels of oxytocin, the "cuddle hormone"), and show mutual care for one another.

Full Love

My own perspective was shaped in the struggle to understand how love is communicated in different types of relationships and, as you might guess, I have been very interested in the love—intimacy connection. As I mentioned

---

3 Susan S. Hendrick and Clyde Hendrick, *Romantic Love* (Thousand Oaks, CA: SAGE, 1992).
4 Robert J. Sternberg, "Triangulating Love," in *The Psychology of Love*, eds. Robert J. Sternberg & Michael L. Barnes (New Haven, CT: Yale University Press, 1988), 119–38; Robert J. Sternberg, *The Triangle of Love: Intimacy, Passion, Commitment* (New York: Basic, 1988).
5 Barbara L. Frederickson, *Love 2.0: How Our Supreme Emotion Affects Everything We Feel, Think, Do, and Become,* (New York: Penguin Group, 2013), 17.

previously, in my younger years, love for my wife, kids, mom, dad, close friends, and even my dog, were forefront in my experience. And, yet, I experienced each of these loving relationships quite differently. This began a journey to find the common essential elements of these diverse loving experiences. And, along the way, I watched for how the various levels of intimacy in each of these relationships related to my love for each individual.

One thing was immediately clear to me regarding the experience of love and intimacy—we can choose to love someone, regardless of her or his response; but we can't build intimacy without the participation of our relational partner. Consider, for example, my relationship with my youngest son, Dan. When Dan was in his junior year he dropped out of high school. As you might guess, this created no small amount of conflict and tension in our family. Dan was pulling away from us in many ways. Ann and I were experiencing fear and stress over Dan's choices, besides the struggle to reconcile our different perspectives as to how to best respond. We joked that our dog Allen was the only person that everyone in our family consistently liked. Yet, in the midst of the confusion and angst, frustration and fatigue, I was well aware of my love for Dan. In spite of the fact that many of Dan's choices had undermined the sense of intimacy that I longed for,[6] I still chose to love him, stay committed to him, and sacrifice for his well-being. And, beyond choice, I maintained a deep sense of emotional connection to him, though the negative feelings that accompanied so many of our daily interactions might have seemed to indicate otherwise.

In this sense, love is unilateral. We can choose to love others, regardless of how they respond or react to our love. We can experience a deep emotional connection with others, regardless of their feelings toward us or, significantly, regardless of our feelings toward them (more on this in a minute). We can even act kindly toward others, choosing a healthy other-oriented perspective, though their behavior toward us is unkind or hurtful. Let's take a closer look at these elements from a *full love* perspective.

The *Model of Full Love* provides what I consider to be essential insights into the messy and rich experience of love in our personal relationships. Full love occurs when we 1) experience a deep *emotional bond* with significant others in our life, 2) *commit* to loving them, and 3) find ourselves taking on healthy *other-oriented* perspectives and actions (even a willingness to sacrifice for our partner's benefit).[7]

---

6 Think of discovery and connection from *Thread 1.5*.

7 The *Model of Full Love* includes aspects of both Sternberg's (intimacy, passion, decision/commitment) and Fredrickson's (emotion-based) ways of understanding love and highlights the essential connection between love and intimacy across different types of relationships. So, I owe my sincere gratitude to these researchers, and others, who have offered keen insight into the process of love.

To gain an understanding of how these three elements might function to create full love, consider a common progression: emotional
bond→commitment→other-oriented focus. Imagine that as you spend
time with a new friend you begin to feel a deep sense of connection to her.
You decide that this relationship is something you would like to pursue
and so you find yourself more committed to her as you allow the sense
of connection to develop into a deeper emotional bond and, importantly,
choose to nurture that bond. Finally, your developing commitment and
emotional connection naturally produce an altruistic relationship frame[8]
that results in other-oriented behavior,[9] such as finding yourself working
to understand your new friend's wants and needs and even making sacrifices for her at times.

Even though it is relatively easy to think of relationships where full
love has seemingly developed in this way, it is important to note that the
development of emotional bonding, commitment, and other-centeredness
is based on reciprocal influence between each element—emotional bonding
creates a sense of commitment, which further enhances the emotional
bond, and so on. In this sense, full love emerges as each love element
influences the others, resulting in a process that is dynamic, but not clean
and neat or sequential.[10]

To appreciate the complexity of this process, consider, Anna, a teen who
found herself unexpectedly pregnant. Anna chose to have her baby, Rosa,
but didn't initially experience much love for the child. Instead, she found
herself overwhelmed by this incredible life "interruption." Nonetheless, she
was committed to Rosa's well-being and sacrificed by getting up at midnight
and 4 a.m. for feedings, changing diapers, delaying high school graduation
until end of summer, and missing out on events with friends when her parents couldn't babysit.

As unexpected as her pregnancy was, Anna soon found herself equally
surprised at the intimacy (discovery and connection) she began to experience with Rosa. This unanticipated closeness was fertile ground for a deep
emotional bond to develop, culminating in a new sense of commitment and

---

8   Relational frames are guiding frameworks that influence how we see our relationships.
Relational frames are, essentially, our relationship worldview (see *Thread 1.1*); Douglas L.
Kelley, *Just Relationships: Living Out Social Justice as Mentor, Family, Friend, and Lover* (New
York: Routledge, 2017).

9   Douglas L. Kelley, "Just Relationships: A Third Way Ethic," *The Atlantic Journal of Communication* (2019).

10 It's important to note that any of the individual elements can be experienced as love, for
instance when one begins to feel emotionally attached to another person. However, full love
only occurs when all three elements are present.

willingness to sacrifice. Anna's care for Rosa changed from mere acts of duty, to wholehearted acts of *full love*. To observe Anna's behaviors, over time, you might notice very little change (for example, she was still getting up at midnight and 4 a.m. for feedings). However, less evident was how her actions had morphed into expressions of commitment, emotional bonding, and other-centeredness.

Unpacking the Elements of Full Love

Each full love element makes a unique contribution to our love experience and warrants a closer look. Let's begin with *emotional bond*. I've chosen this term because it points toward a sense of attachment between partners.[11] In a general sense we experience attachment across relationship type. For instance, I'm definitely emotionally attached to my wife, my sons and their families, and my good friends. What happens to them, and our relationships, affects me at a deep emotional level.

One way researchers have conceptualized attachment is by focusing on infants' experiences with their primary caregivers. An idealistic picture of this could be an infant snuggled in, safe and secure, suckling at mother's breast. Attachment theorists suggest that these early experiences influence our adult views of relationships and connection[12] as we develop "mental models of attachment."[13] These mental models strongly influence our relationship frames and, as such, shape how we see relationships and relationship partners. For instance, infants who receive consistent nurturing learn to view relationships as potentially stable and secure, and are therefore predisposed to build secure attachments as adults. Conversely, infants who experience

11 April R. Trees, "Attachment Theory: The Reciprocal Relationship Between Communication and Attachment Patterns," in *Engaging Theories in Family Communication: Multiple Perspectives*, eds. Dawn O. Braithwaite & Leslie A. Baxter (Thousand Oaks, CA: SAGE, 2006), 165–80.

12 Mary D. Salter Ainsworth et al., *Patterns of Attachment: A Psychological Study of the Strange Situation* (Hillsdale, NJ: Erlbaum, 1978); John A. Bowlby, *A Secure Base: Parent-Child Attachment and Healthy Human Development* (New York: Basic Books, 1988); Charlene Hazen and Peter Shaver, "Conceptualizing Romantic Love as an Attachment Process," *Journal of Personality and Social Psychology* 52 (1987): 511–24.

13 Judith A. Feeney, "When Love Hurts: Understanding Hurtful Events in Couple Relationships," in *Feeling Hurt in Close Relationships*, ed. Anita L. Vangelisti (New York: Cambridge University, 2009), 316.

inconsistent or nonexistent care are more likely to view and create relationships that reflect these same unhealthy tendencies.[14]

Emotional bonding shares important similarities with, and differences from, positive affect (part of the *connection* element of intimacy). Both are related to feeling connected, but intimate experiences are characterized by feelings of closeness and most often positive affect,[15] whereas the attachment foundation of emotional bonding includes, but transcends these elements.

Growing Close 1.7.1

How would you explain to someone what it means to be emotionally bonded? Think about two of your relationships in which you experience emotional bonding. How does the emotional bond in each of these relationships differ one from the other? How is it similar? Is your experience of emotional bonding influenced by your feelings for the other person? (Remember, you can be emotionally bonded with someone whether you are experiencing positive or negative feelings.)[16]

In the previous example with Anna, her early days of motherhood didn't feel "good." She was tired, frustrated, and didn't like many of the responsibilities associated with being a mom. Nonetheless, she found herself becoming deeply connected to her new baby, a connection characterized by a cluster of both positive and negative feelings and experiences.

14 Note that early attachment experiences may predispose you toward a particular relationship style, however, you are not "doomed" to that fate. Over time, other relational experiences, modeling from others, counseling, or even working through the ideas in the book, can lead to transformation of your basic style. See Laura K. Guerrero, "Attachment Theory in Families: The Role of Communication" in *Engaging Theories in Family Communication: Multiple Perspectives*, 2nd ed., eds. Dawn O. Braithwaite, Elizabeth A. Suter, and Kory Floyd (New York: Routledge, 2018), 38–50.

15 In *Thread 1.4* we also recognized that shared negative emotional experiences, especially those that demonstrate commitment to the relationship and understanding, can also facilitate intimacy.

16 See the closing story, in this thread, for an example of this.

Commitment, the second element of full love, is the cognitive choice and investment in a person over time. Emotional bonding, alone, isn't enough for full love. As Sternberg points out, having passion and intimacy in a relationship isn't enough to experience consummate love.[17] Without commitment one might mistake infatuation or lust for love. In addition, research has demonstrated that commitment actually leads to a sort of genuine giving between partners that is associated with higher levels of relational satisfaction.[18]

Importantly, commitment represents the cognitive choice to nurture one's emotional bond—"I like what's happening here. I want to deepen our emotional connection." In this way, commitment also serves to stabilize one's full love experience as long-term. In Anna's case, her commitment to Rosa kept her engaged in the mother–daughter relationship while other full love elements developed.

The third element of full love, *other-centeredness*, emerges from the relational tension that exists between our emotional bonds and choices to commit. Recently, I conceptualized this as a third way[19] process:

> *The tension between cognition and emotion (commitment and emotional bonding) is now seen as dynamic paradox that transcends each individual element and leads to the creation of a third way—other-centeredness— along with a new focus on the transcendent metaphors of altruism, healthy self-sacrifice, healing, and growth.*[20]

Essentially, out of the dynamic paradox[21] that exists between our head and heart, other-centeredness emerges as a third way to see and to act. The beautiful thing about this process is that paradox always values the individual elements of the tension (in this case, cognition/commitment and emotional bonding), but also transcends them. This transcendence is characterized by changing the relationship frames, myths, and metaphors from which we live. For full love this means shifting metaphors from those that focus exclusively on commitment (e.g., love as duty) or emotional bonding (e.g., love as passion) to ones emphasizing altruism, healthy sacrifice, and growth.

17   Robert J. Sternberg, "A Triangular Theory of Love," *Psychological Review* 93 (1986): 119–35; Robert J. Sternberg, "Triangular Theory of Love," in *Encyclopedia of Social Psychology*, eds. Roy F. Baumeister and Kathleen D. Vohs (Thousand Oaks, CA: SAGE Publications, 2007), 998.

18   Scott M. Stanley et al., "Sacrifice as a Predictor of Marital Outcomes," *Family Process* 45, no. 3 (2006): 289–303, https://doi.org/10.1111/j.1545-5300.2006.00171.x.

19   See *Thread 1.3* for more on "third way" processes.

20   Douglas L. Kelley, "Just Relationships: A Third Way Ethic," *The Atlantic Journal of Communication* (2019).

21   See *Thread 1.3* for more on dynamic paradox.

Without the outward focus of other-centeredness, the idea of love runs the risk of becoming narcissistic and self-serving. In other words, an outward focus serves as a check against becoming a "love addict" always seeking the next relational "hit." Instead, being other-centered generates a willingness to sacrifice for our relational partners in healthy ways.

Scott Stanley and colleagues have conducted research demonstrating that couples' attitudes about *sacrifice* influence whether they are happy or distressed, over time, and that sacrifice might actually serve as a system regulator influencing a relationship's potential to fall apart.[22] The key is for sacrifice to be motivated from healthy choices, rather than unhealthy psychological and emotional dependencies. Examples of this are when one partner freely chooses to sacrifice for the other because of a career opportunity, or parents endure financial costs and investment of time to provide opportunities for their children.

What does unhealthy sacrifice look like? Codependence is one example. In codependent relationships each partner's sense of identity and psychological well-being is intertwined with the other's to an unhealthy degree[23]—"I don't know who I am without you," "I don't know how to be happy if you're not happy." "I'm nothing without you." Of course, in moments of crisis we all may temporarily feel these sentiments, but when these ideas permeate a relationship, we have created an unhealthy intimate space.

Growing Close 1.7.2

Think of a time when you became *other-oriented* in one of your significant relationships. How was this other-orientation expressed in healthy ways (e.g., healthy self-sacrifice)? Have there been times that your other-orientation was unhealthy? If so, how can you change this in the future? Are you currently in a relationship that would benefit from a more healthy other-orientation?

---

22 Ibid; Sarah W. Whitton, Scott M. Stanley, and Howard J. Markman, "If I Help My Partner, Will It Hurt Me? Perceptions of Sacrifice in Romantic Relationships," *Journal of Social and Clinical Psychology* 26, no. 1 (2007): 64–91, https://doi.org/10.1521/jscp.2007.26.1.64.
23 Jessica Lampis et al., "The Role of Differentiation of Self and Dyadic Adjustment in Predicting Codependency," *Contemporary Family Therapy* 39, no. 1 (2017): 62–72, https://doi.org/10.1007/s10591-017-9403-4.

In essence, when codependent, my entire well-being is based on something (someone) outside of me, something over which I have no control. In stark contrast, when I have a healthy sense of self-identity (see *Thread 1.5*) I can choose to freely sacrifice for you, because I care for you, not because I need you to be okay in order for me to be okay. The difference here is subtle and can be hard to detect, but is critical to understand as we learn to create *full love* in our relationships.

Full Love: Keeping Intimacy Safe

The crowning characteristic of full love is to create a safe space for intimacy to emerge in our relationships. In a recent article on creating *just relationships*, I argue that, "The dynamic movement between emotional bonding, commitment, and other-centeredness provides the means of creating a safe space for vulnerability and, as such, for intimacy to safely develop."[24] As we have discussed previously, vulnerability is inherent to intimacy. Vulnerability is fundamental to partners' discovery of one another. Yet, we must recognize that it is emotionally irresponsible to make ourselves vulnerable to "unsafe" individuals. Managing this tension (discussed more thoroughly in *Thread 1.6*) between desiring intimacy/vulnerability and wanting to remain emotionally safe is a constant struggle in our relational lives. But, full love provides a means of securing our personal and relational well-being.

When students ask me how they can know if they should make a long-term commitment to a relationship, I ask them questions to gain a better idea as to whether or not they are experiencing *full love*. Are they deeply attached to one another? Are they seriously committed to each other? Are they willing to sacrifice in healthy ways for each other? Are they committed to the vulnerability that being discovered entails?

Considering these questions is as close as we can come to safeguarding our hearts. To take this approach intentionally recognizes that each full love element (emotional bonding, commitment, and other centeredness) represents an essential aspect of our healthy relationship tool box: the ability to securely attach emotionally and psychologically to another person, the cognitive ability to make a commitment, and the ability to act in altruistic ways in response to relationally nourishing attachment and commitment.

---

24 Douglas L. Kelley, "Just Relationships: A Third Way Ethic," *The Atlantic Journal of Communication* (2019).

Intimate Reflections

Earlier in this conversational thread, I told the story of my youngest son, Dan, and the ability to choose to love even when times are tough. I'd like to share another event in that love story as we tie together some final thoughts.

Late one evening, around midnight, I received a phone call—the name of Dan's close friend, Ramsey, appeared on my phone. My first thought was that Dan had forgotten his own phone and was using Ramsey's to have me let them in the house, so I was a bit irritated at having been roused from a sound sleep. But upon answering the phone, instead of hearing Dan's apology for having wakened me, I heard Ramsey's voice echoing through the small phone speaker, "Dan's been in an accident. It's bad. He was thrown from a car." My heart sank. Actually, "sank" isn't even close to what I felt. My heart plummeted to the depths of my emotional ocean. Even writing these words, some ten years later, I can feel my visceral response—racing heart, watery eyes, sweaty palms, paralysis. I shook my head. My mind was spinning out of control. This couldn't be happening to us. I choked out to Ann, "Dan's been thrown from a car. We need to go."

A couple of hours later we stood in the ICU at Dan's bedside. He was bloody, oxygen tubes protruding from his nostrils. Unconscious. Future ... uncertain. All the hardship, frustration, and anger that we had been experiencing at that time no longer mattered. The emotional bond I had maintained, and the commitment I had continued to choose, usurped those past feelings. Instead, wildly loving thoughts manifested themselves as I stood helpless next to my son. "We have a lifetime to spend together." "I should have been able to protect you." "I would do anything to turn back time." Attached. Committed. Sacrificial. Full love.

Transformation Through Discovery, Connection, and Being

This is the final thread of our opening conversation about intimacy. Hopefully this conversation has offered new insights, brought some surprises, and stimulated questions to keep pondering. For me, it has meant immersing myself in various social science perspectives, engaging my students over rough drafts of each of these threads, and long days and nights sifting through my own thoughts and experience of closeness with others. Undoubtedly, my thinking is still in process. However, I am confident that certain ideas that we've discussed here will remain fairly stable over time. I end this conversation with one such idea: *true intimacy brings individual and relational transformation.*

Let's begin exploring the idea of transformation by retracing where we have been together. We began thinking about personal relationships as intimate spaces characterized by interdependence, synergy, resilience, depth, synchronicity, and each partner being recognized and treated as a "person." We asked the question, "Is it possible that we are made for intimacy?" and then acknowledged that our relationships are in a constant pull between closedness (privacy) and openness, autonomy and connection. This led us to explore the paradoxical nature of intimacy—we desire autonomy and yet hope to be connected to other individual persons.

We then explored intimacy as discovering others, being discovered by others, and the connection we feel when that discovery is embraced. It turned out that curiosity is key to unearthing our own sense of self and discovering our relational partners.

We grappled with the idea that vulnerability is a natural part of discovery and connection and that without it there is no deep sense of intimacy. Then, the essential question: What is to be done regarding the vulnerability risk inherent in relationship- and person-building? Trust, courage, and curiosity all play a role. But, as trite or corny as it may sound, apparently, love is the answer. We found that full love, characterized by emotional bonding, commitment, and other-centeredness (including healthy sacrifice), creates a safe space for vulnerability and, thus, for intimacy. Which brings us to our present discussion—the experience of intimacy is always transformative.

Perhaps the retelling of where we have just been has made it self-evident—the nature of discovery is to be introduced to new information and novel experiences that necessitate some type of response. Some type of adaptation. Some type of change. New friends share a bottle of wine and talk into the night, each continually reassessing their relationship and individual selves as new information is revealed. A couple marries and two years into the process realize that their idea of who they thought they were marrying at the altar doesn't fully exist—time for some adjustment. A parent laments changes in her wayward 13-year old daughter, "Where did my sweet little girl go? I don't know her anymore," and is challenged to reconsider her own self and relationship to her daughter. A good friend shares a "secret", told in confidence, and now the friendship must be reassessed in light of what has been learned about the "trusted" friend. During a rather playful, unguarded moment, romantic partners drop some of their defenses—they are thankful for this new relationship place, but afraid of their newfound vulnerability. As these examples demonstrate, being in relationship with others challenges us to reconsider our partners and our own selves. Discovery and connection within relationships take us to places that we will never discover alone and, thus, are transformative by nature.

How does this transformation take place? Each of the preceding situations could be handled in ways that don't precipitate significant change, so what makes the difference between transformation and status quo? The answer lies in the connection between mindfulness and intimacy. The commonalities between these two processes, or states of being, offer insight into the transformative nature of intimacy, and the necessary discovery of one's self.

Valerie Manusov describes mindfulness as follows, "be aware of, and accept without judgment, experiences as they exist in the present moment."[1] Let's unpack the key elements of this definition with relation to intimacy. Awareness—to know or be known, to discover. Present moment—to be *with* another person[2], to experience a sense of connectedness in a particular moment. Acceptance without judgment—to have an other-oriented focus (judgment presumes a focus on one's own perspective) and as such create a safe relational space. Manusov goes on to say, "The point is this, if we become more mindful (in the sense that we encourage awareness, being present, and not judging), we can be more fully with another person and ourselves *just as we are*"[3]. In essence, mindfulness is a means of cultivating intimacy and connection.[4] But, let me take this even further. More fully with others and ourselves presumes that *we actually discover others and ourselves more fully.* In essence, we transform our relationships and ourselves by becoming more aware of ourselves and others. This insight is not lost on Manusov, as she goes on to state, "Acting with mindfulness, being curious rather than confident about the meaning for behavior, allows ... for new information to arise, for learning to happen, for unexpected opportunities to emerge."[5]

In this sense we see that mindfulness encourages curiosity, discovery, connection, and transformation. However, being mindful doesn't make intimacy happen. Rather, it creates a space for intimacy to emerge. In the introduction to this book, I use the analogy of intimacy, like a butterfly, seeming to randomly choose when and where to land. In reality these choices are not random for the butterfly, nor for intimacy—certain conditions create spaces where both of these elusive marvels flourish. Choosing to be mindful in our interactions creates space for intimacy to emerge, to grow, to land on our relational noses.[6]

A final note about *transformative intimate moments.* As my research staff and I combed through participants' intimacy stories, the word *moment* kept

---

1 Valerie Manusov, "Mindfulness as Morality: Awareness, Nonjudgment, and Nonreactivity in Couples' Communication," in *Moral Talk across the Lifespan: Creating Good Relationships,* eds. Vincent Waldron and Douglas Kelley (New York: Peter Lang, 2015), 191.

2 There are also mindfulness practices that focus on being present to oneself, rather than to another person.

3 Ibid, 196.

4 It is important to recognize, as does Manusov, that mindfulness is not always used for connection.

5 Ibid, 196.

6 In *Conversation 3* we explore a number of expressions of this type of intimate space.

popping up. It was clear that many participants didn't associate intimacy simply with specific behaviors (for example, sex or talk). Rather, there was something unique and special about moments where intimacy emerged. Certainly, feelings were involved, but there was much more. Not unlike Manusov's "present moment," these intimate moments were often reported as transformative experiences, such as when individuals experienced closeness, worth and value, openness and vulnerability, presence with another person, as well as the freedom to *be* one's "true self."

Our second conversation, *Myths that Inhibit Discovery, Connection, and Being*, explores certain beliefs about intimacy that, if left unchecked, potentially rob us of the transformation our intimate moments can bring. And, in what may seem a counterintuitive move, in the last thread we spend some time experimenting with *true myths* that can actually help us create the intimate spaces we desire.

Conversation Two

*Myths that Inhibit Discovery,
Connection, and Being*

Thread 2.1

Relationship Myths

'm thinking about costumes and ghosts and spooky situations. Yes, I see the obvious connection here—relationships can seem scary and ephemeral—but it's also Halloween today and I'm pondering how powerful popular myths can be. The idea of myth has come to be primarily associated with that which we no longer hold to be true—ghosts, Zeus, George Washington never telling a lie. But myths only survive because there is some element of truth to them.

This second *Intimate Spaces* conversation has to do with relationship myths. It focuses on ideas that can limit our experience of intimacy. It recognizes that all of these ideas feel "true" to us, in one sense or another, or we wouldn't keep hold of them. And, yet, each thread of conversation in this section will also suggest ways to transcend limitations inherent in the myths themselves. For instance, while many of us have experienced what we consider to be gender differences in our relationships, to simply categorize all women as relational, and men as not, limits our potential to engage one another. Transcending these types of simple categories and beliefs can open us to fuller understandings of what it means to be in relationship.

In this spirit, each thread of this conversation explores a prevalent intimacy myth, but then makes a resolve to go beyond that myth. You'll be encouraged to adopt new resolves such as being willing to handcraft your relationship, to become more your "self" through intimacy, to actually "show up" and be present with your relational partners, and to expand your intimacy repertoire.

Intimate Reflections

Myths are powerful because we tend to live in ways that are consistent with what we believe. If you think of yourself as athletic, you may be more likely to work out in the morning or after work than if you are simply trying to lose weight. If you see yourself as compassionate, you will more likely respond to others with mercy and grace than if you are simply doing what you think you "should." In essence, we tend to move our lives toward that on which we are focused. I think of this much like driving a car at night on a desolate highway – you find yourself consistently moving toward the centerline because it is most salient in your visual field.

We can use this basic tendency to build stronger, more intimate, relationships. If you will, we can paint our centerline where we want it. If you think of your relationship as one characterized by talk, or play, or shared activities you are more likely to live in a way that makes those "myths" come true. As such, this second conversation encourages you to live into the positive relational myths you co-create with your partner.

Thread 2.2

Myth: I want intimacy

Resolve: I will put energy into creating handcrafted, intimate relationships

never thought my wife and I would need marriage counseling. After all, I teach this stuff! However, I'm grateful to report that, for us, counseling opened some deep pathways to intimacy. During this time I was surprised at the hard questions I had to ask myself. This wasn't really about learning some new skills. This was about changing perspective and deciding what I really wanted.[1]

During a private session with our therapist a most significant question presented itself. At one point Pam sat back in her chair, looked at me, and asked, "Do you want to be in this relationship?" I was blindsided. How could she even ask that? Of course I wanted to be in the relationship! Didn't I? I came to realize that I had never really given myself permission to think that ending our marriage was a legitimate option. As such, the question haunted me—Did I want this relationship? Once home, I couldn't get this off my mind, but it soon morphed into something even more poignant: "Do I really want intimacy?" Again, "Of course I do! Don't I?" As I looked back over the history of our marriage, I began to wonder. I had made many choices to keep things positive in our relationship and to keep us both happy. Nothing wrong with that.

---

1 By the way, Ann says the same for her experience, as well.

But, it slowly became evident to me that I used many of these "good" things to avoid what I like to call *the hard work of intimacy.*

Do We Really Want the Hard Work of Intimacy?

Consider how the following statements may indicate a desire to avoid intimacy:

> "This is getting too close, for me. I'm out!"
> "Do we have to talk about everything?"
> "If I tell him how I feel, I risk losing him."
> "Can't we just go back to 'normal'?"
> "If a relationship is meant to be, shouldn't it be easier than this?"
> "I just feel too hurt to work on this."
> "We're nice. We're comfortable. Can't we just let it be?"

Most of us have said or thought one or more of these statements in one relationship or another. The statements aren't wrong. In fact, they represent much that's true about our emotional state at any given time—"I'm emotionally drained," "I'm afraid," "I'm hurting." However, if they become *go-to* responses they may represent resistance to doing intimacy's hard work.

In two research studies that I've conducted with long-term romantic couples,[2] I have heard over and over that marriage takes work. No surprise there. But, social media and television often give the impression that there are quick fixes to most relationship problems. In sharp contrast, listen to a couple of research participants from a study I conducted with colleague and friend, Vince Waldron. First, a husband emphasizes the importance of knowing what you want in the long run and then choosing to act in ways that makes that happen:

> *Marriage is work. You've got chores to do. I think at any time you can look at these things and ask, "What the hell did I do this for? I was living pretty good at home" (laughter). But if you really look at the long haul, your marriage can work out. It's just, step up and do your job. That's it.*

---

2 Douglas L. Kelley, "Understanding Relational Expectations and Perceptions of Relational Satisfaction in Marital Relationships" (PhD diss., University of Arizona, 1988); Vincent R. Waldron and Douglas L. Kelley, *Communicating Forgiveness* (Thousand Oaks, CA: SAGE, 2008).

> ## Growing Close 2.2.1
>
> Do you really want intimacy? Are some of your thoughts and actions actually being used to avoid intimacy? Go through the previous list of statements that can be used to avoid intimacy. Add your own to the list. How might you change these statements to reflect a desire to grow in intimacy in one of your relationships?

Maybe not the most romantic view of marriage, but a smart emphasis on not losing sight of the "long haul" as you make choices in your relationship. One of our participant wives also emphasizes keeping a larger perspective as she stresses changing behavioral patterns and perspectives:

> *I really have changed. He's changed, but so have I, and if you want to work at marriage you don't have any choice. I have learned not to push his buttons at times. We used to fight a lot. ... Now I evaluate what's important in life.*

Both of these statements underscore that the hard work of intimacy involves making choices to act and think in new ways that are consistent with "what's important in life." This is not easy. It's tempting to think, "I like who I am. And, I just want you to fit into my life as it is." No work, just a good fit. This, however, is an unrealistic perspective, as we'll discuss later in *Thread 2.8*. One of our husband participants articulated pretty clearly what I'm trying to say:

> *I mean, you're putting two people together with maybe totally different backgrounds [and] personalities, and you know you're not going to agree on the same things always. It's something that you want to work at in order to make it better.*

Metaphors for Building Intimacy

I recognize that focusing on the *work of intimacy* may take the magic out of it. But let me offer two alternative metaphors, to *work*, that may just put back the magic. In our recent book on conflict, forgiveness, and reconciliation, Vince Waldron, Dayna Kloeber, and I suggest that using metaphors to imagine change is a powerful way to transform our relationships.[3]

One possible relationship metaphor is, *running the race*. I'm a runner of sorts. I used to street run and now primarily do short stints of trail running. I've heard non-runner friends make the following comment as we drive past a pathetic figure trudging uphill midway through their morning routine, "He doesn't look like he's having any fun. Not for me!" But that perspective misses the point. Anyone who has worked hard to gain a particular skill knows that there can be great joy in difficult moments, if those moments are leading toward something that is important and highly valued.

A second potential metaphor is *team*. Intimacy involves two individuals working together to discover and connect. The work of intimacy can't rely solely on individual effort. As we discussed toward the end of our last conversation,[4] love can be unilateral (I can love you regardless of your response to me), but intimacy requires two persons—without two, there is no reciprocal discovery and connection. Take a look at the following quote from one of our husband participants:

> *What we're committed to is we're committed to two people to become one. I interact with her to make this thing work so that both of us benefit and neither one of us suffers any more than we have to. So I think all of this comes out of a mental commitment that we're going to make it work.*

I particularly love his statement, *so that both of us benefit and neither one of us suffers any more than we have to*. In some ways, that is realistically what it means to be in an intimate relationship—working together so that each of us benefits and we reduce suffering for both partners.

Intimate Reflections

We have been exploring the idea that the intimacy many of us want is one without the hard work required. Running and team metaphors shed new light on what it might mean to work on intimacy in a relationship, but let me

---

3 Douglas L. Kelley, Vincent R. Waldron, and Dayna N. Kloeber, *A Communicative Approach to Conflict, Forgiveness, and Reconciliation: Reimagining Our Relationships*, (New York: Routledge, 2019).

4 See *Thread 1.8*.

Growing Close 2.2.2

Do the metaphors of *running the race or team* resonate with you as ways that you can choose intimacy? If so, how might embracing one of these metaphors change the way you pursue intimacy in one of your relationships? Might they affect what you are looking for in a relationship partner? If not, what metaphor would be useful to move one of your relationships toward more discovery and connection?

throw one more metaphor into the mix before we move to the next thread of this conversation. In each of my studies where participants talked about long-term relationships as being *work*, there were always couples who said that their relationships actually hadn't been any work at all. When I first heard these statements I thought, "You are either crazy, a saint, or married to a saint!" But that wasn't the point they were trying to make. Actually, they were offering an alternative perspective on what it takes to do a relationship well. Much like any craftsperson would describe a beloved project, these happy relational partners thought of their relationships as requiring exertion, determination, and effort, rather than "work." They realized that it takes energy to make a relationship work!

Since his retirement, my brother-in-law, Scott, has become quite an accomplished woodworker. When he created new kitchen cabinets for his home, was it a lot of effort? Absolutely. Did it take a lot of determination and focus? You bet. But when you love something you're doing, the effort you put in doesn't always feel like work. Scott tackled his project with a level of energy that kept him focused on his long-term goal of producing quality cabinets for his home. So, I offer *energy*, as an alternative relationship metaphor. Scott's handcrafted cabinets required a lot of energy, but not necessarily a lot of "work." And, both the process and the result were definitely worth it! Are you willing to put in the energy it takes to create a handcrafted intimate relationship? How might your relationships change if you approached them knowing that intimacy is not going to come easy?

Thread 2.3

Myth: I don't need intimacy

Resolve: I will be open to filling my intimacy hunger

There are some great reasons to avoid intimacy in our relationships. Do any of the following statements sound familiar?

"Intimacy scares me to death."
"Relationships shouldn't be that much work."
"Too vulnerable!"
"Intimacy just sounds like more obligation."
"Constricting!"
"I will never be hurt like that again!"
"I was taught not to need anybody. I'm my own person."

I get it. As we talked in the last thread, I've had to ask myself if I want to do the hard work of intimacy. I've wondered, do I have the energy for intimacy? Is it worth it? And, I'm definitely with you as to not wanting to be hurt. I'd rather protect myself by being my own person, doing my own thing. But, in spite of these reasons, I have chosen to pursue intimacy. And I think there are compelling reasons for you to consider the same.

We Are Drawn to Intimacy

As we discussed in the opening conversation of this book, we are indeed made for intimacy. This aspect of our humanness continually draws us toward other persons. Of course, many of us have well learned to shut down this response, but even the fact that we have to shut down the desire for closeness confirms our basic longing for connection.

Take a look at my rather gruff step-father, Roger, who liked to put on a tough exterior. He was a "self-made" man who took charge of any situation when given the chance. I knew he cared for me, but he wasn't going to show it through nurturing. He liked to bark out orders and watch others fall in line. Glimpses of his soft side, however, surfaced when least expected. For instance, Roger constantly bad-mouthed our miniature dachshund, Prince—he was useless, temperamental, and pooped on the carpet (Prince, not Roger). One day, Roger, underwear clad (tighty whities, nonetheless!), even chased Prince through the house with a broom, trying to get him to go to the backyard.[1] Yet, periodically Mom and I would catch Roger sitting on the couch, gently petting Prince as he lay next to Roger's leg.

This amusing anecdote reflects findings by the PEW Research Center that examined perceptions of closeness versus distance in a variety of relationship types.[2] When asked about their pets, 94% of dog owners reported their relationship with their dog as *close*, compared to 84% of cat owners. And, get this. When adults were asked the same questions about their parents, 87% reported their relationship with their mom as close, whereas only 74% of respondents used the word "close" to describe their relationship with their dads. In case you missed this, let me make it even clearer—the rank order of relationships that feel close is as follows: dogs, moms, cats, and ... dads! As a dad, I find this a bit discouraging. But, I have to admit that I'm not surprised.

Of course, there are good reasons that dogs come out on top. Go back to the list, at the beginning of this thread. The reasons not to be in an intimate relationship don't apply to dogs and cats: closeness doesn't seem frightening or too vulnerable, the obligations are generally pretty straight forward, you don't worry about getting hurt in the relationship (at least until your beloved pet dies), your pet doesn't ask you to change, and you can be your own person.

---

1 My mother later joked that we learned to never again buy a cheap broom as pieces of straw were flung all over the house!

2 Paul Taylor, Cary Funk, and Peyton Craighill, "Gauging Family Intimacy: Dogs Edge Cats (Dads Trail Both)," retrieved from Pew Research Center: Social Trends Report, http://assets. pewresearch.org/wp-content/uploads/sites/3/2010/10/Pets.pdf.

Growing Close 2.3.1

Make a list of those with whom you have experienced closeness in the last few weeks. The focus here is on your experience of closeness. I'm not asking whether you talked deeply or spent a lot of time together, rather consider when and with whom you have experienced a particular moment as feeling close. This can include people who are physically distant, are no longer living, friends, family, lovers, and even pets. Does the list surprise you in any way? Are you content and happy with this list?

The point is this: whether it is with mom, dad, dog, or cat, most of us are in relationships that feel close in some way. In fact, another study by the PEW Research Center found that in spite of our mobile society, 73% of people surveyed reported each day being in touch with a family member who doesn't live in their house. Evidently, we desire connection.

The Need for Affection

Researcher Kory Floyd,[3] has suggested that many of us find ourselves in a condition he terms *affection hunger*. Affection hunger suggests that we are not getting the amount of affection from others that we desire or expect. In this regard, a recent study by CIGNA,[4] using the University of California, Los Angeles' Loneliness Scale, found that nearly half of Americans (47%) report sometimes or always feeling alone. Importantly, the report concludes that, "People who engage in frequent meaningful in-person interactions

3 Kory Floyd, *The Loneliness Cure: Six Strategies for Finding Real Connections in Your Life* (Avon, MA: Adams Media, 2015); Kory Floyd, "Relational and health Correlates of Affection Deprivation," *Western Journal of Communication* 78, no. 4 (2014): 383–403, https://doi.org/ 10.1080/10570314.2014.927071; Kory Floyd, *Communicating Affection: Interpersonal Behavior and Social Context* (New York: Cambridge University Press, 2006).
4 "Cigna U.S. Loneliness Index," MultiVu, accessed June 26, 2019, https://www.mul-tivu.com/players/English/8294451-cigna-us-loneliness-survey/docs/IndexReport _1524069371598-173525450.pdf.

have much lower loneliness scores and report better health than those who rarely interact with others face-to-face."[5]

Floyd highlights how, in many ways, *affection hunger* is like regular hunger—we need both food and affection for survival; we feel bad when we don't get these things, good when we do; and, deprivation of both leads to health complications and unhealthy compensatory behavior. He then suggests six strategies for meeting our affection needs. For our purposes, let's look at four of these strategies to overcome loneliness.

First, *be open to receiving affection.* It may be that you're signaling a reluctance to receive affection through your hesitation to engage in intimacy. In other words, your fear or self-protective posture may be indicating to others that you are not interested in going deeper in your relationship or that you don't want to be close. This of course can become a self-fulfilling prophecy. That is, you behave in ways that facilitate the very outcome of which you're afraid. For instance, you may maintain distance in a relationship because you're afraid you'll get hurt. Your partner then pulls away because she senses your closedness. Consequently, you feel hurt (which confirms your original fear) and pull away farther to protect yourself.

Second, *invite and model the type of relationship you seek.* This follows from Floyd's first suggestion. That is, instead of signaling that you are closed and protective in the relationship, decide to model the openness you seek. A consistent finding in relationship research is that we tend to reciprocate like behaviors—if you share something, I share something; if you move closer, I move closer; if you are negative, I am negative. So, to some degree, you can set the tone for the level of affection or talk or negativity that you want. In addition, Floyd's use of the term, *invite,* is well chosen. As we have discussed, relationships are spaces into which people are invited, and within which they co-create their intimate experience. Of course, this means risk and vulnerability—your invitation may go unnoticed or unheeded. Yet, as we discussed in the previous conversation, with safe partners, vulnerability is often worth the risk.

Third, Floyd encourages us to *recognize diversity in affection displays.* That is, affection doesn't take only one shape or necessarily look like what you are expecting. A useful example of the diverse ways in which affection can be shown is the idea of *love languages,* a term popularized by counselor and author, Gary Chapman.[6] The basic premise of love languages is that

5 "New Cigna Study Reveals Loneliness at Epidemic Levels in America," MultiVu, accessed June 26, 2019, https://www.multivu.com/players/English/8294451-cigna-us-loneliness-survey/.
6 Chapman, Gary D. *The Five Love Languages: How to Express Heartfelt Commitment to Your Mate* (Chicago: Northfield Publishing, 2004).

we all have different ways we like to give and receive love. In other words, behaviors communicate different meanings for each of us. Some receive love more effectively through words. Others gifts. Some touch. Some time. Others through acts of service. The key is knowing what says "affection" to your relational partner, and knowing what means "affection" to you.

The fourth of Floyd's strategies is to nurture a variety of affectionate relationships. The bottom line here is, no one person can provide all of your affection needs. When Ann and I were first married we attended a young-marrieds' class at a local church. I still vividly remember a guest speaker saying, "Your spouse is not going to meet all of your needs." What?!!! It's embarrassing to me now, but I truly didn't know this. I had been putting too much pressure on Ann with my expectation that she meet all of my needs. This expectation had also led me to neglect some of my close friendships. Floyd encourages us to take stock of where we are getting our affection and to nurture those relationships. Then, cultivate new relationships that don't threaten the old.

Intimate Reflections

Twenty-five years ago when Ann and I returned to our home town, I left my closest friend, Dick, behind in Seattle. Over time I developed other male friendships, but I didn't feel like I needed a lot of friends in Phoenix because my friendship with Dick was still strong. There also didn't seem to be many good candidates in Phoenix for *New Best Friend*. However, when Dick died several years later, he left a huge hole in my life. Crazily, I was also in counseling with Ann during that time. Who would have thought that my two closest friends would be unavailable to me at such a crucial time—Ann was unavailable to help me process Dick's death, Dick was unavailable to help me process my marriage. At that point I had to make an assessment of the various elements we've just been discussing. I decided I was open to going deeper with the friendships I had. *I became open to filling my intimacy hunger.* As I got together with a couple of these friends, I began to model the openness and vulnerability that I needed from a friend at that time. Thankfully, my friend Mike responded. It was a huge risk when I told him what Ann and I were going through and I opened up to him in a way that left me pretty vulnerable. And? Surprise! Guess who could go deep when the door was opened? That's right. Mike.

Thread 2.4

Myth: You can lose your "self" in intimacy

Resolve: I will become more my "self" through others

C an you lose your "self" in intimacy? You bet. But not in the way you might think. Intimacy, when understood as a space of discovery and connection, demands discovery of our true selves. And, ironically, what we saw in the previous conversation is that discovery of self comes primarily through connection with others.

My research team for the *Intimacy in Personal Relationships* (IPR) study found that respondents consistently discussed specific intimate behaviors and specific intimacy themes based on their experience. For instance, when respondents identified a specific behavior associated with intimacy, such as deep talk, they often also described their experience of that behavior as it was associated with relational qualities such as trust, safety, or feeling understood.

One stand-out experiential theme we labeled, *True Self*. People told us that in their most intimate relationships they were free to be their true self or free to discover their true self. One of our respondents made explicitly clear that, "Being your true self with someone else who is their true self," is the essence of intimacy. This was expanded upon by others. For instance, one respondent reflected that intimacy is, "Being comfortable enough with one another to just be your true self, and laugh and make jokes. These simple moments helped to create something much bigger [in the relationship]." Another told us,

> *Being my true self has created intimacy because you are allowing someone to know you on a different level than others. You can take*

off the mask and be you. When you are silly and having fun you find a different [kind] of love for someone.

I think my favorite *true self* response is this one:

To me, intimacy means being so close to somebody that you are able to reveal your true and vulnerable self to them. I experience intimacy during deep and emotional conversations with friends, family, and my partner and during lovemaking with my partner as well. Being fully attentive to another person exclusively for a moment of time is how I view it.

We'll discuss the last part of this quotation in a later thread, but here I want to emphasize that intimacy is not losing yourself, rather, it is revealing "your true and vulnerable self" to others, and perhaps to your own self, as well. Let's take a closer look at this perspective.

Changing Our Relationship Frame: Viewing and Doing

A few years ago, I would regularly ask a counselor friend of mine, Bill, to be a guest speaker in my family communication course. Bill spoke often to community groups and had a standard way of presenting his perspective on healthy relationships. One class session he unexpectedly changed up his usual lesson and said, "I used to view relationships as the overlapping space between two individuals. Like two circles overlapping one another. I now prefer a model that emphasizes the connection between two healthy individuals."

I had already been shifting my own relationship frame[1] away from the overlapping circle perspective on relationships, and Bill's comments forced me to think more critically about what could be unhealthy about viewing relationships this way. Later, for one of our campus clubs, I spoke about healthy and unhealthy relationships, and presented my new thinking about relationships by using the following graphics (my original art, by the way!). They are overly simplistic, but I think they do the trick to get us thinking about changing our mindsets regarding the nature of relationships and intimacy.

We begin with Figure 2.4.1, two happy individuals interested in beginning a relationship. Figure 2.4.2 illustrates the way many of us have traditionally understood our relationships: two separate individuals overlapping part of

---

1 As noted in *Conversation One*, relationship frame is the lens with which we view our relationships. How we frame our relationships influences how we see our relationships and, subsequently, how we do our relationships. Thus, the phrase—viewing and doing.

their individual "selfs." In Figure 2.4.3, we start to see the problem. Notice in this picture that both individuals begin to lose their essential identities. They are no longer two individuals connecting and finding a sense of their "true" self. Rather, they have morphed into something that is less recognizable (and, unfortunately in this case, that turns smiles into some type of creepy moustache!).

One of the consequences of this way of viewing and doing relationships is evident in Figure 2.4.4—when the partners go their own separate ways, each partner is left less whole than when they started. Rather than having grown and become more their true self during the relationship, they have become something they hardly recognize now that they are out of the relationship. In this way, unhealthy connection, such as co-dependence ("I need you, in order to be me") often shows its true colors during breakups, leaving us wondering if we'll ever feel whole again.

FIGURE 2.4.1

Most of us can probably relate to this experience of relationships—when I'm with you I'm more outgoing, more energetic, less neurotic ... more *me*! In fact, we discussed this as synergy, in *Thread 1.3*. It's the wonderful, often surprising, effect that can occur in close relationships. Yet, healthy relationships must be built on two healthy individuals. In this sense, relational intimacy is first dependent on each individual being separate, unique. Only then, can the synergy that results from bringing together these two separate entities (partners) lead to the eventual emergence of intimacy.

FIGURE 2.4.2

FIGURE 2.4.3

In this regard, consider Figure 2.4.5. Granted, it's a bit unrealistic, but it gets the point across and is a rather fun perspective! Here, two whole selfs have intertwined their lives together. It is a bit messy,[2] but both selfs are whole and, because they are whole, they are more likely to come to the relationship as emotionally and psychologically healthy individuals, better able to co-create a healthy

FIGURE 2.4.4

---

2 Truth be told, one of the reasons I love studying relationships is that they are messy!

FIGURE 2.4.5

FIGURE 2.4.6

relationship. The relationship has enhanced each partner and they have become oriented one toward the other.

Figure 2.4.6 demonstrates that the impact of a breakup on two whole individuals is less likely to be as devastating. The two may even remain friends or acquaintances, or at least part without hating each other.

I want to reemphasize that these drawings reflect my early thinking about shifting our relational frames. The final two drawings are in no way meant to assume that if we are healthy individuals we will always walk away from relational endings with smiles on our faces. However, the usefulness of these drawings is that they help us begin to shift our thinking from "*I need this relationship to be whole*" to "*through this relationship I can grow and become something closer to my true self.*" In this light, let's take another look at discovery and connection.

Growing Close 2.4.1

Is it a new idea for you that personal relationships are spaces where you should grow and become your true self? If so, do you have relationships where "losing yourself" has been a concern? What kinds of changes might help you and your relational partners connect in healthier ways and grow into your true selfs?

Discovery and Connection

Our opening conversation discussed intimate relationships as spaces characterized by discovery and connection. As we have been discussing, the nature of discovery requires two distinct individuals. Consider that if we are not distinct from one another, at least in some ways, there is nothing to discover. When two distinct selves give access to one another informationally, socially, physically, and psychologically they become co-owners of their various intimate spaces.[3] And as a result the two distinct relational partners find themselves connected.

I have heard countless individuals state that they know themselves, better than anyone else can know them. And while there is truth to that statement, it's a misnomer to think we "know" our own self completely. We need connection with others to discover who we really are. Not so that we become like others, but that through them or with them, we better understand our most intimate self and are able to make decisions to pursue or allow becoming and change.

Essentially, the challenge is for each of us to create and preserve awareness and openness to what our relational partners have to teach us through modeling, nonverbal responses to our behavior, and verbal conversations. I remember a time when Daniel (my youngest son), Ann, and I were in a pretty intense conversation. I finally proclaimed, "That's it. I'm done. I have nothing left to say," and started to leave the room. Daniel quickly spoke up, "That's what you always do. You leave when it's not easy." I looked at Ann, "Is that what I do? I leave when things get hard?" She nodded, "Yup." Wow. Blindsided. I'm collaborative, aren't I? Evidently not. Turns out I'm a huge avoider. Thankfully, I stayed to finish the conversation. But, equally important is that I had moved closer to what I consider to be my true self—through my son's words, in that rather intimate conflict space, I became more of a collaborator that day.

A few years ago, my cousin's daughter, Tiffany, created a drawing for me to illustrate a relationship frame that emphasizes two healthy individuals engaged in the creative act of *becoming* as they balance a relationship with one another (see Figure 2.4.7). In her drawing you see that the relationship (all that is balanced on their heads), rather than being represented as the overlap of two relational partners, is its own separate entity—the outcome of two autonomous persons connecting. The relationship only exists with the presence and participation of both individuals, but at the same time, is also independent of them. Tiffany's drawing highlights many of the varied elements that may be part of a couples' relationship. In this drawing they face each other, but we can also imagine a time when these partners are going through disappointments and frustrations and are turned away from one another, but still supporting the relationship.

We may also consider, as we did with my previous drawings, what happens if this couple breaks up. Clearly, during relationship dissolution there could be significant challenges negotiating the management of their

---

3 See *Thread 1.4*.

co-created intimate space. However, because the individuals are left as whole persons, though possibly bruised and injured, they will be able to manage their relationship termination or transformation cooperatively and with grace.

FIGURE 2.4.7

Fig. 2.4.7: Created by Tiffany England, at www.tiffanyengland.com.

Intimate Reflections

Key to the perspective represented in *Figure 2.4.7* is two partners, equally matched, in balance—without which many aspects of the relationship come crashing to the ground. A vital focus of the relationship is for each partner to stay healthy, growing, and becoming—together. As such, we make the resolve—I will become more my "self" through others.

English philosopher, David Whyte, alludes to this process when he states, "There is no self that will survive a real conversation."[4] This provocative statement makes evident that real encounter brings about real change. Intimacy through discovery and connection can lead to personal transformation. This means the fear that we will lose our sense of self, if we give our self to intimacy, is well founded. But, not in the way most people think, being swallowed up by someone else larger than ourselves. Rather, we may lose the self we've been clinging to, as we more fully discover who we are.

---

4 David Whyte and Krista Tippett, "The Conversational Nature of Reality," April 6, 2016, in *On Being with Krista Tippett*, podcast, https://onbeing.org/programs/david-whyte-the-conversational-nature-of-reality-dec2018/.

Thread 2.5

Myth: Intimacy is something you do

Resolve: I will practice "showing up" in my personal relationships

Perhaps this "myth" caught you by surprise. What else is intimacy, if not something you do? Maybe you're wondering how I, as a communication professor, could undercut my own academic pursuits by implying that intimacy is not behavior?

The next three threads challenge the idea that intimacy is something we "do," as if talking more, spending more time together, and learning a few new sexual techniques each creates intimacy in and of itself. Like many myths, the belief that certain behaviors are synonymous with intimacy has some element of truth in it, but misses the mark. To be clear, what we do in our relationships is critically important. However, *our perceptions and experience of those behaviors is* what ultimately determines whether or not something is considered intimate by relational partners. Consider the potential negative impact of each example at the beginning of this paragraph: talking more can be experienced as TMI (too much information!) rather than deepening, spending more time together can be suffocating rather than connecting, and, certainly, sex can be hurtful or seen as a duty rather than emotionally bonding.

To explore the myth that intimacy is something you do, let's look at how *audience analysis* helps us understand what counts as intimacy and how relationally *showing up* can create the discovery and connection we are hoping for.

What Counts as Intimacy?
Understanding Your Personal Audience

The word "audience" is generally associated with groups of individuals listening to a particular speaker or mediated message. In truth, audiences exist in both public and interpersonal contexts. During an interpersonal interaction your audience is simply your relational partner. And like larger audiences, our partners (interpersonal audiences) play an active role in the communication process as they interpret behaviors that they perceive as being communicative and respond verbally and nonverbally to these "messages." This transactional part of the communication process—mutual influence throughout all our face-to-face interactions—is the key. It's not just what we do, but how that "doing" is perceived.

Effective communicators and performers recognize the importance of knowing their audience in order to craft messages that facilitate understanding. A simple example of this process occurred quite a few years ago when my oldest son, Jon, was about 10-years-old. I was upstairs working and called down to Jon for some help. The conversation went something like …

"Jonathan, can you bring me the book that is on the arm of the couch in the living room?"

"Sure, Dad."

Moments later, Jon calls out, "It's not there."

"Yes, it is. It's on the arm of the couch."

"I don't see it."

"It's there. Look on the ARM OF THE COUCH IN THE LIVING ROOM!"

"Nope. Not there."

At this point I get up and walk into the upstairs hallway that overlooks the living room. Jon's not there (but I see the book on the arm of the couch!). "Jon, where are you?"

"Sitting on the couch in the living room."

At this point, I realize my mistake (sigh), "Jonathan, you're not in the living room, you're in the family room."

"Oh." Then, he pops into the living room with a smile, "Hey, here's your book Dad!"

What happened here? Poor audience analysis. I didn't think about the fact that my audience (Jon) didn't know the difference between the living room and family room. *I continued to send a message that worked for me, not for him.* This is a common problem in close relationships—we assume our partners assign meaning to messages in the same way we, ourselves, assign meaning. Consider a former student of mine who was frustrated with his wife. Stefan, maneuvered his wheel chair into my office one day and asked if we could talk about his new marriage to Andrea. His litany of complaints gushed out like water released from an open hydrant, "I do all of these wonderful things for my wife. I clean the kitchen, I put gas in her car, I regularly bring her flowers, I pick up her favorite foods from the store, and I make the bed. But, she doesn't seem to appreciate it, and then is frustrated with me if I don't sit with her to watch TV in the evening!" Of course there are a couple issues that could be going on here, but one that seems evident is poor audience analysis—they each have different ways of showing care and experiencing intimacy. For Stefan, acts of service and gifts are meaningful, for Andrea it's spending time together by watching her favorite television shows.[1]

Being audience-focused allows us to be "good" or competent communicators as we fashion messages that are ethical, situationally appropriate, and effective in achieving mutually beneficial goals.[2] Because we are goal-oriented creatures, part of communicator competence is sending messages that achieve our end goals through clarity and influence. But, we are also relational creatures, so sending ethical and situationally appropriate messages is essential, safeguarding us from communicating in ways that are controlling or manipulative or insensitive.

Ethical and appropriate communication is based, in large part, on understanding the rules that operate during any given interaction. Consider, for example, two types of rules that guide our conversations. *Regulative rules* regulate how things are done in the relationship. Regulative rules might include whether it's ok to kiss in public or how to handle conflict.

Constitutive rules determine what something counts as or represents. In other words, constitutive rules tell us what something means, within the context of a given interaction. These rules might include agreeing on what counts as respect or love or meaningful time together. Not too long ago I was talking with Joe, who was struggling in his first year of marriage: "Regina values time together so I spent an entire Saturday with her cleaning and rearranging our apartment. Later, when I asked if we could go together to

---

1 Note our discussion in the previous thread regarding *love languages.*

2 Brian H. Spitzberg and William R. Cupach, *Handbook of Interpersonal Communication Competence* (New York: Springer-Verlag, 1988)

a group event that night, she said, 'We haven't had any *us* time.' It blew my mind. I mean, we had just spent eight hours of *US* time!" For Regina, getting work done together was important, but it didn't constitute or *count as* intimacy. For Joe, his intimacy cup was filled and he was ready to hang with friends. As a competent communicator, Joe's job became clear—to understand what *counts as* intimacy for his personal audience, Regina, and help her understand what counts as intimacy for him.

Growing Close 2.5.1

Take a moment to consider what *counts as* intimacy for you. Now, think about one of your relationships (friend, family, lover). What *counts as* intimacy for that relationship partner? Don't limit yourself to fixed categories on this. For instance, as you'll learn in *Conversation Three*, play often *counts as* connection and intimacy for me. This was something Ann had to learn. On the other hand, giving Ann an affectionate hug when she comes home from work can say "intimacy" to her. What is it that you and your relational partners experience as intimate?

Mindfully Showing Up

As you heard in the first conversation, I've come to believe that certain aspects of mindfulness form the foundation for much of what we *count as* intimacy and that mindfulness is essential for healthy personal and relational growth. Finishing this thread, I want to explore mindfulness as relationally *showing up*.

In order to cope with life's various challenges, all of us have learned ways to protect ourselves by not showing up—even though physically present, we avoid connection through distraction, changing the subject, and emotionally disengaging.[3] In contrast, practicing mindfulness allows us to be present and aware with another person—and even ourselves—without judgment. As I

---

3 Douglas L. Kelley, *Just Relationships: Living Out Social Justice as Mentor, Family, Friend, and Lover* (New York: Routledge, 2017).

quoted previously, Manusov suggests that when mindful, "We can be more fully with another person and ourselves *just as we are*."[4]

Let's briefly revisit the idea that mindfulness (presence, awareness, and nonjudgment) shares much in common with intimacy. Presence, for our purposes, can be thought of as presence with another human being, that is, *showing up* physically, emotionally, mentally. This type of presence produces a deep sense of connection and closeness as your partner senses that you are focused on what is happening *now* with him or her.

Awareness is exercised by taking note of your partner and yourself. Curiosity can be a healthy way to think about this. Rather than primarily thinking about how to respond to your partner, awareness can begin with a curious attitude. Here we engage our senses as we observe our partner's behaviors and our own internal response. What might my partner be feeling or trying to express? How am I emotionally, physically, or psychologically responding and what might that tell me?

Of special note here, questions such as these can serve as a means of becoming more aware, but take care that the questions don't actually distract from being *present with* the other. For me, personally, I can get so lost inside my head during a conversation that I lose any sense of *being with my* relational partner. Because of this, when I ask questions I try to focus on ones that request elaboration ("Tell me more about how you felt?" "Keep going with how you responded to your boss"). This allows my partner to participate in determining the direction of the conversation, to tell me what they want to tell me rather than what I want to hear. I also practice taking note of what's happening in a conversation, while taking only minimal time to process it. I often analyze it later, but during the conversation I keep my analysis to a minimum and try to focus on being curious and observant.

Finally, mindful awareness is bereft of judgment. There is a time and place for analysis and evaluation, but this is not it. For now, I am aware of you! As one of our research participants put it, "Aware of the 'good and bad.'" But, aware without judgment. Safe. As we discussed in our opening conversation, being known and accepted by another human being creates safe space to be vulnerable and aware of our worth and value. Further, these are the conditions that lead to eventual transformation, the discovery and expression of one's true self. In this way, being mindfully present in our relationships is a means of allowing one's true self to emerge ... to show up.

---

4 Valerie Manusov, "Mindfulness as Morality: Awareness, Nonjudgment, and Nonreactivity in Couples' Communication," in *Moral Talk across the Lifespan: Creating Good Relationships*, eds. Vincent Waldron and Douglas Kelley (New York: Peter Lang, 2015), 183–201.

Intimate Reflections

In *A Communicative Approach to Conflict, Forgiveness, and Reconciliation* I wrote about the emotionally focused therapy (EFT) that my wife and I encountered together.[5] The focus of our therapy was on the emotions experienced and expressed in session (the *now*), rather than spending time analyzing what happened during the previous week. To be honest, I often did not want to go because getting in touch with my emotions was difficult for me. I really didn't want to *show up* emotionally. Other forms of counseling we experienced focused on identifying a problem and solving it. I'm all about that. Identify the problem, analyze the problem, brainstorm, and implement solutions. Conquer the problem!

Fortunately, as difficult as the process was for me, I deeply valued and was committed to our choice of EFT, and it proved to be highly effective. Our sessions were often unpredictable and out of my control. I remember a session where our therapist, Pam, asked me a question and I was giving her a good left-brain response—logical and detached. As I was talking, Pam asked me how I thought Ann felt about what I was sharing. I hadn't been looking at Ann, because I was responding to Pam's question, so I said, "I don't know. I suppose it doesn't feel good, but it's something we have both acknowledged so I am guessing she is fine with it." Pam gently prodded, "Take a look at your wife." When I turned toward Ann, I saw tears welled up in her eyes. How could I possibly have been so unaware of how Ann might feel about what I was sharing? I, a communication professor, was oblivious to what my statement would "count as" to my relational audience (Ann). Her tears brought me back to the moment—present and aware, without judgment. I had been lost inside my head. It was time for me to finally *show up*, head and heart, to our counseling sessions.

So, intimacy isn't just the things we do. Intimacy is predicated on how our partners experience those things we do. In this sense, we have to become mindful communicators, focusing on understanding our interpersonal audiences. Let's review what this means: *presence with* becomes connection, awareness becomes discovery, and *without judgment* becomes a safe space for vulnerability and the true self. Is there a relationship you need to *show up* to today? In the following two chapters we are going to continue this theme as we discuss showing up in our gendered and sexual relationships.

---

5   Douglas L. Kelley, Vincent R. Waldron, and Dayna N. Kloeber, *A Communicative Approach to Conflict, Forgiveness, and Reconciliation: Reimagining Our Relationships* (New York: Routledge, 2019).

Thread 2.6

Myth: Women are better than men at intimacy

Resolve: I will expand my intimacy repertoire

sat quietly, listening to Jan, a 22-year-old in tears over a break up. The couple had planned on waiting to have sex until married, but their desire for each other, along with the belief that that they were soulmates[1] and would never break up, resulted in a sexually active relationship. Now, after encountering significant conflict as the relationship developed, Jan was crushed at having lost "true love" as well as betraying the vow to "wait until marriage." Jan was disoriented, mildly depressed, and dealing with a significant amount of guilt and shame.

A few years later I listened to Alex tell me of "breaking it off, just when the relationship was good," to avoid being hurt. Alex was effectively leaving a trail of broken relationships and broken potential partners along way. There was a little guilt about all of this, but Alex never promised anyone that the relationship would last any longer than it did: "If they got their hopes up, I feel badly for them, but it's really not my problem. I told them not to get hooked."

Every time I ask a group, "What's your experience? Are men and women different in how they communicate?", many people emphatically respond, "Yes!" But, as these opening examples reveal, it's not always easy to predict how men and women act in their relationships. In the

---

1 More to come on this in *Thread 2.8*.

opening scenarios, did you think Jan and Alex were male or female? Many of us would assume that Jan was female, crying over the loss of a soulmate, and Alex was male, interested in sex but afraid of commitment. Yet, in reality, these true examples were just the opposite—Jan was a young man in the police academy and Alex a female working with a non-profit organization.

We exist in a world that often uses psychological gender (e.g., feminine-masculine) and biological sex (e.g., female and male anatomy) as descriptors of people and things. Take for example certain languages that have masculine (el camino—the road) and feminine nouns (la comida—the food), plumbing fixtures that are either male or female based on whether the piece is being screwed into or doing the screwing (I'll let you draw your own conclusions from this example), and cultural norms that dictate what it means to be a man (action/task-oriented, decisive, rational) or a woman (relational, nurturing, emotionally expressive).[2]

The perspective that male–female communication differences are both prevalent and important, largely comes from culturally-based messages and a few common experiences that appear to confirm certain cultural norms. Yet, we must recognize that none of us perfectly fits these common perceptions. For example, Ann and I relate to certain popular speakers and writers who discuss male–female differences, because in some ways we fit many of these classic stereotypes—I'm typically less in touch with my emotions than she is and I get more frustrated than she does when I can't control things in my life. Yet, we do not fit common stereotypes in other ways—she is much more independent than I am and more of a "fixer" in relationships.

Casual interpretation of social scientific research has also led to confusion regarding the effects of gender and biological sex on communication choices and, in particular, how we "do" intimacy. For instance, social scientists have discovered statistical differences between men and women in affiliation motivation[3] and expression of affectionate behavior,[4] however these differences don't preclude that men, or those who possess a sense of masculinity, desire intimacy. To this very point, Floyd reports that while

---

2 The Bem Sex Role Inventory classifies masculinity as including ambitious, assertive, analytical, dominant, and self-reliant, and classifies femininity as including affectionate, cheerful, gentle, loyal, compassionate, soft spoken, and understanding. Sandra L. Bem, "The Measurement of Psychological Androgyny," *Journal of Consulting and Clinical Psychology* 42, no. 2 (1974): 155–62.

3 Amely Drescher and Oliver C. Schultheiss, "Meta-Analytic Evidence for Higher Implicit Affiliation and Intimacy Scores in Women, Compared to Men," *Journal of Research in Personality* 64 (2016) 1–10, http://dx.doi.org/10.1016/j.jrp.2016.06.019.

4 Kory Floyd, *Communicating Affection: Interpersonal Behavior and Social Context* (New York: Cambridge University Press, 2006).

masculinity is typically less associated with affection than femininity, both masculinity and femininity are positively associated with the expression of affectionate behavior.[5] Others have maintained that, whatever differences exist between men and women, they generally don't have as great an impact on relationships as we might think.[6] The bottom line is, individuals matter. However gender and biological sex generally influence one's expression and experience of intimacy, we still need to understand how these elements work themselves out with our partners and within our relationships. Let's take a look at three guidelines that help frame issues of gender and biological sex and expand how we think about intimacy.

Using Gender and Biological Sex to Expand Our Intimacy Repertoire

I find the following three perspectives helpful in negotiating the relational landscape of gender and biological sex. Of particular note, these perspectives can be used to create a sense of mindful awareness and presence that leads to acceptance and transformation, rather than judgment, division, and misunderstanding. I recently presented these in one of my classes and we had a wonderfully productive discussion. I hope they provide stimulating and useful thoughts for you, as well.

First, let's consider the idea that making generalizations is essential to our being human. Our brains naturally look for patterns in data and then generalize from those patterns. Every time you flip on a light switch you are operating from a generalization you have learned, either from an authority you respect, by observing this particular pattern, or from repeated experience—switches "generally" turn things on and off. You may not know the physics of electricity, but you have made a generalization that has served you well.

Relationally, you make similar generalizations all of the time. For instance, when you go to a job interview or meet your romantic partner's parents you make certain educated guesses, based on generalizations, about how to

---

5 Ibid.
6 Peter A. Andersen, "Researching Sex Differences within Sex Similarities: The Evolutionary Consequences of Reproductive Differences," in *Sex Differences and Similarities in Communication*, eds. Daniel J. Canary and Kathryn Dindia (Mahwah, NJ: Lawrence Erlbaum, 1998), 83–100; Laura K. Guerrero, Peter A. Andersen, and Walid A. Afifi: *Communication in Relationships*, 4th edition (Thousand Oaks, CA: SAGE, 2016).

behave. The key is to *use generalizations as points of curiosity and discovery and to hold them lightly*. For instance, when listening to your friend Amanda talk about Brandon's insensitivity, you can allow your generalization—men are out of touch with their emotions—to stimulate your curiosity: I wonder if Amanda is referencing Brandon's failure to respond to her emotional experience in the relationship or if it had to do with something else? Or, perhaps you've made a generalization that gay men are emotionally sensitive. Knowing that Brandon identifies as gay, you might wonder whether Amanda holds that same generalization. If so, you can explore whether her expectations (Brandon should be emotionally sensitive) are contributing to her frustration. If not, you can explore other possibilities and also consider altering your generalization that gay men tend to be more emotionally sensitive.

The key is to resist the temptation to turn your generalizations into blanket stereotypes. Instead, become more aware of your generalizations and hold them lightly and mindfully while being curious and open to change.

A second perspective is to recognize that, however you identify in terms of gender and biological sex, there is much to learn from others. I've gained perspective on this from my practice of T'ai Chi. The focus on mind/body connection and balance has been particularly interesting to me. T'ai Chi emphasizes the balance between yin and yang energies.[7] Central to this practice is the recognition that both yin and yang are needed for peak performance and human development. Yin is passive virtue that can be exhibited as patience, kindness, sentiment, and worry, whereas, yang is active virtue often exhibited as progressiveness, intelligence, joy, and anger. Note that both are virtues. Both are necessary. In fact, to only develop one aspect of this dynamic tension can be dangerous. For example, emphasizing kindness (yin), to the exclusion of intelligence (yang), leaves one vulnerable with a potentially unsafe other. From a T'ai Chi perspective, one seeks a "harmonized union of yin and yang energies" (p. 40). T'ai Chi practitioners must develop each of these elements in order to move toward their full potential.

For students of relationships (which I hope we all are), learning from each side of the gender divide (our relationship yin and yang) can help us grow into a fuller sense of intimacy that might, otherwise, elude us. For instance, a focus on personal sharing (classic feminine approach to relationships) certainly can facilitate wonderful discovery of one another's psychological and emotional intimate spaces, but exclusive focus on sharing misses out on other ways of knowing and being present with other persons. Likewise, activity (classic masculine approach to relationships) provides an important

7 Hua-Ching Ni and Mao Shing Ni with Joseph Miller, *Tai Chi for a Healthy Body, Mind and Spirit* (Los Angeles: Tao of Wellness Press, 2011).

means of discovery through observation of one's partner while working or playing. But exclusive dependence on activity and observation can lead to misinterpretation of relational messages or completely missing certain aspects of our partner's experience.

Thankfully as intimate partners we can embrace a rich variety of means to communicate. Through donning a learning attitude, we bypass simplistic ideas that regard intimacy as something that is either talk or activity and instead focus on discovery and connection through both what we say and what we do.

The third perspective that I find beneficial is transcendence of the masculine–feminine tension. As a friend of mine recently put it, we need to guard against, "... over corrections. There are differences, and they are important, but at the same time it's important not to have a dualistic mind-set."[8] We can at times transcend the dualistic tension experienced within gender and biological sex (masculine-feminine, male-female) by adopting a *third way* mindset.[9]

Think back to our *Thread 1.7* discussion where I conceptualized *full love* as a third way process. With full love, the dynamic tension (or dynamic paradox) that exists between cognition (choice and commitment) and emotion (emotional bond as attachment), results in a third way perspective shift—other-centeredness—that values, but transcends the tension.

We can obtain this third way experience regarding gender, as well. Our experience of tension between female and male, masculine and feminine, can result in a third way outcome—our shared humanity—that transcends these tensions. From a third way perspective, we can appreciate and learn from both feminine and masculine experiences, but the overall perspective shifts from the constant push and pull between this gendered dichotomy (Am I feminine, enough? Am I masculine enough?), to questions that transcend the gender tension (Am I becoming more fully human? Am I helping others embrace their full humanity? Am I finding and expressing my true self?).

In interpersonal interactions, some individuals choose to use personal pronouns, such as *them* and *they*, to try and transcend dualistic understandings of gender and biological sex. Others avoid traditional pronouns (her, him) or simply try to remain open as they engage each individual encounter. However individuals try to manage the limitations of language when it comes to gender and biological sex differences in their daily lives, third way process shifts our relationship narratives and metaphors from strictly dualistic

8 Conversation with Dr. Ted Wueste, April 20, 2019.
9 Douglas L. Kelley, "Just Relationships: A Third Way Ethic," *The Atlantic Journal of Communication* (2019). DOI: 10.1080/15456870.2020.1684290. Also, see *Threads 1.1* and *1.7.*

images (feminine–masculine, male–female, he-she) to images of transformation through presence, growth, development, becoming, and unity. Imagine deciding to be more or less nurturing, not because nurturing is or is not feminine, but rather because you want to learn to be more other-centered and to care for other human beings!

Growing Close 2.6.1

What if you adopted a new perspective regarding the effects of gender and biological sex in your intimate relationships? Do you have generalizations that you need to let go of or alter? What is it you can learn about intimacy from your partner? Can you look for a third way perspective that shifts your focus to what makes you and your partner most human? Will you commit today to expand your intimacy repertoire?

Intimate Reflections

In this thread we have touched on the complicated issue of how psychological gender and biological sex influence our experience of intimacy. We have looked at generalizations we all make and how to keep them from turning into incalcitrant stereotypes. We have focused on learning from the other, however the other construes herself or himself or themself. And we have explored what it means to transcend dualistic perspectives regarding gender and biological sex, exploring how third way process reorients us to metaphors associated with our shared humanity.

As we close this thread regarding biological sex and gender, I offer a final story about transcendence. A graduate teaching assistant of mine a few years ago identified as bi-sexual, although her romantic relationships were primarily lesbian in nature. I didn't know anything about her sexual orientation when she began working with me. She was simply, Chelsea—bright, fun loving, hard working. And she was incredibly liked by the students. One day for class she lectured on language bias. In that lecture she shared phrases that had been said by other people about her and her relationships, including, "Who is the man and who is the woman in the relationship?"

It was a very moving class as students asked questions and processed their own biases. As they realized that Chelsea's choice to identify as bisexual was part of her own journey to find her true self, her story now had become part of their journey, too.

Thread 2.7

Myth: Sex is intimacy

Resolve: I will be mindfully present during my intimate sexual encounters

A few years ago, I was asked to give a short lecture to a group of graduating high school seniors who had been admitted to Arizona State University and invited to experience a day of college life. At the time I was teaching a class on relational communication and we were in a segment that focused on intimacy. I thought, "If there is one thing high school students will be interested in, it's intimacy!"

When I entered the classroom that day I began with the question, "What is intimacy?" They looked at me with bright eyes and ... silence.

But I was ready for them, "Okay. What would it mean if I asked you if you had been intimate with your boyfriend or girlfriend?"

You guessed it. Silence, again. Until one young man sat up in his seat and said, "Sex. You'd be asking if we'd had sex." He looked pretty proud for having said "sex" in a college classroom!

"Exactly," I replied. "But let me ask you this. Is all sex intimate?"

Suddenly, 12 of these previously silent students called out, "NO!"

"Ah," I followed, "then what is intimacy?"

A prevalent myth is that sex and intimacy are synonymous. In my relational communication course I address this myth by asking my students to interview friends, family, and coworkers about their perspectives as to what intimacy is or what it means to me intimate in a personal relationship.

Equally revealing are the responses I received from *IPR* participants.[1] To the question, "Please describe a time where *sex* has demonstrated or created intimacy in one of your relationships," a number of individuals told us they hadn't experienced intimacy during sex because they weren't yet sexually active, while others stated that their sexual activity had never created or demonstrated intimacy. Clearly, people engage (or not) in sexual activity for a variety of reasons. However, our interest here is in how sex can function as a means of creating and expressing intimacy.[2]

We're Having Sex Here. Do You Mind?

The last two conversational threads have focused on viewing intimacy as something we experience, rather than a concrete skill set that we implement or "do." In a certain sense we are always *doing* something, however, it is essential that we examine the question: How are we *being*, when we are *doing*?

If your desire is to have a more fully intimate sexual experience, you have to set aside the idea that sex is simply something physical. You must also determine to be beautifully *mindfully present* with your relational partner.

One of my *IPR* participants put it so well when she stated:

Sex has created a sense of trust within my relationships. It shows that I am comfortable enough with you to let you see me at my most vulnerable. ... Sex is a soul tie so whenever I take that step with someone I am letting them in and giving them the chance to hurt me.

Let's take a look at this rather profound perspective on sexual experience through the lens of mindfulness. Previously we have considered mindfulness as being present and aware without judgment.[3] The participant quoted above recognizes presence during a sexual encounter when she uses the word "with" and ultimately describes sex as a "soul tie." This soul tie experience involves awareness, letting her partner "in" to see her when she's most vulnerable. She's willing to be vulnerable because she has created a relational space characterized by safety, trust, and nonjudgment.

---

1 *IPR* references the Intimacy in Personal Relationships Study.
2 See *Thread 3.4* in *Conversation Three* for more on this.
3 Valerie Manusov, "Mindfulness as Morality: Awareness, Nonjudgment, and Nonreactivity in Couples' Communication," in *Moral Talk across the Lifespan: Creating Good Relationships*, eds. Vincent Waldron and Douglas Kelley (New York: Peter Lang, 2015), 183–201.

Think back to our first conversation where I characterized intimate relationships as safe spaces where good things can happen. When we are willing to be mindfully present with our partner during sex, we have the opportunity to create a relational space that is profoundly affirming and connecting. You and I connect as you "see me at my most vulnerable," do not judge, and want to be with me, here and now. And, of course, I do the same with you.

Growing Close 2.7.1

If you are sexually involved with someone, does it sound appealing to be *mindfully present* for your partner and for your partner to be *mindfully present* for you during sex? If so, how can you help create a safe place where you and your partner can become more present and aware with one another?

Brené Brown, states that even married couples often feel vulnerable when engaging in seemingly simple requests, such as, requesting sex from their spouse.[4] Is emotional vulnerability, as it relates to sexual aspects of your relationship, working to create a "soul tie" between you and your partner or, instead, causing you to pull away and protect?

Intimate Reflections

Let's finish this thread by looking at how lessons from public speaking and singing might improve our sexual experience. As a communication professor, I have taught my share of public speaking classes. One of the things I love about teaching students to communicate publicly is that public speaking is very much tied to who we are as persons. Why else would individuals report speaking in public as their greatest fear, even more than dying?[5] At least dying,

---

4 Brené Brown, "The Power of Vulnerability," filmed June 2010 at TEDxHouston, Houston, TX, video, https://www.ted.com/talks/brene_brown_on_vulnerability#t-12244.
5 Karen Kanga Dwyer and Marlina M. Davidson, "Is Public Speaking Really More Feared Than Death?" *Communication Research Reports* 29, no. 2 (2012): 99–107.

I guess, can be thought of as escape. With public speaking you are stuck ... alone ... in front of a live audience, exposed with all of your imperfections.

One of my favorite comments to write to a student regarding his or her speech is, "Where did you go?" This wonderfully bright, engaging student suddenly disappeared as he or she began "giving a speech" and we were left with the technical accuracy of a well-constructed outline. When lost in technical accuracy, speakers lose the ability to connect with their audience.

In this same vein, last night at rehearsal (my wife and I sing in a semi-professional choral ensemble[6]) our director cajoled us, "Don't wear your technique on your face!" In other words, some of us were so busy singing the notes and dynamics with accuracy that we missed what was happening in the music and failed to engage the audience.

When *you*, the "person," disappear, so does any possibility of intimacy with you. "Where did you go?" is a great question to ask as you contemplate your sexual experience. Just as public speaking reveals something about you, so can sex. Are you so caught up in the activity of sex, or sexual technique, or the "duty" of sex, that you forget to show up? Or maybe you can't let go of work or other responsibilities or even your phone and so are never really here, *now*, with your partner. When we approach sex as a "soul tie"—a safe space where we can be *mindfully present*—it becomes a beautiful place of discovery and connection.

That said, experiencing sex and intimacy as a "soul tie" can have its own downsides when we overly idealize what soul tie represents. In the next thread we take a closer look at mythic elements of finding your soulmate.

---

6 Learn more at SonoranDesertChorale.org.

Thread 2.8

Myth: Intimacy is about finding your soulmate

Resolve: I will work with my "mate" to co-create a relationship that nurtures our souls

"You complete me!" This classic line from Jerry McGuire represents the essence of what many think of as finding your *soulmate*—I'm incomplete until I find ... YOU. For many of us, this makes perfect sense. Possibly, we have been in a relationship like this or, maybe, if we are lucky, we're still in that relationship.

On the other hand, let's think for a moment of less healthy perspectives that might accompany our soulmate beliefs: "I will never be complete on my own." "There is only one person in the world for me" (and by implication, if I miss finding that person, I'm relationally doomed!). "As soulmates, we are so perfectly matched that we will never have deep conflict." "A soulmate relationship shouldn't require effort."

Clearly, if we find ourselves falling into this type of thinking, we can be setting up our relationships for potential problems. So, let's take a moment to unpack the idea of soulmates, the good and the bad.

Soulmates

The term, soulmate, combines two words—*soul* and *mate*—to describe a type of relational partner. In this sense, soulmate refers to finding a mate (a pairing or companion or partner) for one's soul (one's inner-most being). It connotes a relationship that is "meant to be."[1] But, more than that, the idea of soulmate is really intended to highlight one's experience of a "special" relational partner. This is pretty close to the *Oxford Dictionary Definition* of soulmate: "A person who shares a deep understanding or bond with another; *esp.* one ideally suited to another as a lover or spouse."[2] This definition emphasizes being suited to, understood, and bonded with. Not a bad way to think about what it might mean to be, or find, a soulmate.

However, the idea of soulmate is frequently confused with a number of unhealthy ideas. For instance, believing we should be "ideally" suited to another person may set us up for unrealistic expectations. Think about your friend who wants to get married after six months of dating, "We never fight. We are just so compatible. He can virtually read my mind! We have such a great 'vibe' together."

Soulmate experiences are influenced by a sense of compatibility, or fit, that may be triggered through synchronicity.[3] There is something naturally attractive when we find ourselves in sync with others. I personally believe this is one of the key factors in strong early attraction. Recently, a friend of ours after only one date exclaimed, "This guy is the one!" Well, unfortunately, it turned out he wasn't the one. However, much of what she experienced as being the "one," was not so much matching on an online dating profile, but rather feeling "in sync" on their first date. Everything seemed to flow, seemed natural, went without a hitch, and this created a strong sense of attraction.

Interestingly, we experience this on the flip side, as well. When a couple is struggling in their relationship, they often feel out of sync with the other. The simplest conversations suddenly seem difficult—"I just said, it's ... in ... the ... bottom ... drawer." "Seriously? How do you not know that I like garlic?"

The bottom line here is that synchronicity feels wonderful when we experience it with another person, and is actually an important sign of possible compatibility. But synchronicity isn't a guarantee of long-term compatibility, nor is the lack of synchronicity to be taken as a singular sign that a relationship should end. I'm reminded of a research participant who, when asked the benefits of a long-term relationship, quipped, "Oh my gosh!

---

1 Rachel M. Reznik, Michael E. Roloff, and Courtney Waite Miller. "There is Nothing as Calming as a Good Theory: How a Soulmate Theory Helps Individuals Experience Less Demand/Withdraw and Stress," in *Communicating Interpersonal Conflict in Close Relationships*, ed. Jennifer A. Samp (New York: Routledge, 2016), 39.

2 *Oxford English Dictionary* (Oxford, UK: Oxford University Press, 2019).

3 For more on synchronicity see *Conversation One*.

I would never want to have to train someone new to live with me!"[4] In essence, we are all going to have moments where we feel out of sync, but ... "this one's pretty well trained!"

In contrast to a perspective that infers soulmate relationships should primarily be easy (in sync) and happy, American poet laureate, Ralph Waldo Emerson, tells us that true friends are, at times, nettles in our side. With great eloquence and insight, Emerson writes of the beauty and balance of friendship ("mates" or partners)—each partner maintaining her or his own sense of self while engaging the other in such a way that unity is eventually discovered:

> *Better be a nettle in the side of your friend than his echo ... There must be very two, before there can be very one. Let it be an alliance of two large, formidable natures, mutually beheld, mutually feared, before yet they recognize the deep identity which, beneath these disparities, unites them.*[5]

Emerson substantiates what we've been discussing throughout our conversations, that intimacy is based on two healthy individuals discovering each other's "deep identity," and developing a profound sense of connection that embraces and acknowledges obvious differences. As I have mentioned previously, this to me is the beauty and magic of intimacy—it is a third way process wherein unity is discovered in the midst of difference, rather than by eliminating or remaining blind to our dissimilarities.[6]

A rather interesting approach to understanding the idea of soulmates, the *Soulmates Model*,[7] provides a holistic perspective on long-term relationship development. Seventeenth century pictograms are used as visual references, and the seven-stage model culminates in soul mating completion, flourishing, and sustainability.

I find the last three stages of the model most interesting. The first four stages are what one might expect: dating, commitment, intimacy, followed by building a life together. However, stage five, *Integrating the shadow, rising from the square* (imagery from the pictograms), might be surprising to some. In this stage, the authors smartly recognize that building a life together

---

4 From research conducted by my colleague, Vince Waldron, and myself—Vincent R. Waldron and Douglas L. Kelley, *Communicating Forgiveness* (Thousand Oaks, CA: SAGE, 2008).
5 Ralph Waldo Emerson, *Essays, First Series* (Auckland, New Zealand: The Floating Press, 2009), 180.
6 See *Thread* 1.8 for more on third way process.
7 Luisa Batthyany De La Lama, Luis De La Lama and Ariana Wittgenstein, "The Soulmates Model: A Seven-Stage Model for Couple's Long-term Relationship Development and Flourishing," *The Family Journal* 20, no. 3 (2012): 283–91, https://doi.org/10.1177/1066480712449797.

provides ample opportunity to discover differences, to inadvertently or purposefully hurt one another, or simply to stall out emotionally and lose a sense of meaning in the relationship.

Stage six follows this shadow time with *renewal* and is characterized by the development of new meaning and purpose with rebuilt love and care. Stage seven, *soul mating completion, flourishing, and sustainability*, continues these efforts with a focus on steering away from what is unwanted and creatively moving toward what is desired.

Importantly, beginning with stage five, *integrating the shadow*, the model stipulates that there is a growing recognition of a crisis requiring relational partners to commit to a cause that transcends all else. In this way, much like our discussion of suffering in *Conversation One*, soul mating is ultimately dependent upon shared transcendent meaning that only emerges from struggle in the relationship.

I frequently ask my students, "Why should we maintain relationships over the long haul?" The fact that transcendent meaning can emerge through struggle is one of the reasons. Of course, struggle doesn't guarantee transcendence, but it provides opportunity for new and deeper meaning to emerge in our relationships. In the early days of my marriage, I prided myself on how similar Ann and I were. Years later I was stunned when Ann told me, "I'm not going to just say 'yes' to you, all the time, any longer." What?! Is that what has been happening all these years? Obviously, this created a new struggle for us, but great life came out of that struggle as Ann more fully found her voice in our relationship, and a deeper transcendent meaning materialized as we more honestly engaged one another—truer soulmates than we were before.

In a previous thread I mentioned that my wife and I sing in a semi-professional choir. For the last concert of this academic year we performed, *Amor de Mi Alma*, by Z. Randall Stroope,[8] with text by Garcilaso de la Vega. This poem from the Renaissance era seems a fitting follow-up to the *Soulmates Model*, as it represents a beautiful tension between healthy and unhealthy perspectives. Originally penned in Spanish, de la Vega's luscious poem can be translated:

> *I was born to love only you;*
> *My soul has formed you to its measure;*
> *I want you as a garment for my soul.*

---

8 Another ASU graduate. I highly recommend listening to a recording of this piece from the Spanish Renaissance.

Your very image is written on my soul;
Such indescribable intimacy
I hide even from you.

All that I have, I owe to you;
For you I was born, for you I live,
For you I must die, and for you
I give my last breath.

De la Vega's perspective on love and intimacy begins in the first stanza speaking to closeness in purpose, formation of being, and connection. The opening line, "I was born to love only you," certainly comes with its risks (what if you're already taken or my love is unrequited?), but also reflects the intimate experience of the lover—I have purpose in loving you.

"My soul has formed you to its measure" acknowledges the role of perception, as well as the potential influence of each partner on the growth and development of the other—in this intimacy we are both becoming.

"I want you as a garment for my soul" speaks of the desire for connection, not suffocating, but like a garment that colors, protects, and keeps warm.

The second stanza strikes at the beautiful sense of vulnerability we have discussed as an essential part of mutual discovery. The lovers are deeply known by one another, *"Your very image is written on my soul."* At the same time, they are overwhelmed, ecstatic, and frightened. *"Such indescribable intimacy, I hide even from you."* They are deeply knowing and being known.

The final stanza strikes to the core of the relationship between intimacy and love. Such mutual becoming has created a sense that I owe who I am to you and want to live my life in a way that is sensitive to your needs and desires. *"All that I have, I owe to you; for you I was born, for you I live, for you I must die, and for you I give my last breath."*

As we look at this romantic poem it's easy to see the potential downsides— codependence, my identity totally dependent on my partner, lack of a healthy sense of self to bring to the relationship, idealizing one's partner to such an extent that no one can live up to. But, if we stay aware of these potential pitfalls, we can use the idea of soulmate to keep us deeply emotionally connected with our partners, focused on mutual discovery, becoming, connection, other-centeredness, and purpose.

Intimate Reflections

I finish this thread with a 20-year-old story from one of my students. JoAnn had returned to school after some difficult personal times, including divorce and single-parenting a rebellious teenage son. Her research project for my class focused on the benefits of maintaining long-term romantic relationships.

One day, standing in the checkout line at her local grocery, she struck up a conversation with a forlorn looking man in his 70s. When the conversation turned to her schooling, she shared about her research.

"What does it mean to be in a long-term relationship?" asked the older gentleman. "I'll tell you what it means. It means that I can't eat toast in the morning, any longer."

JoAnn looked at him quizzically.

With tears in his eyes, he finished, "My wife passed away a month ago. Every morning I would put bread in the toaster and, when toasted, she would take it out and butter it. I simply can't have toast any longer."

The metaphor of making toast is a power picture of soul mating. Not to be missed, however, is that though he could no longer have his morning toast he was still able to get out of bed and go to the store. And, although I don't know what happened with this man, his story reminds us that life with our soulmates doesn't just prepare us for life together, it equally prepares us for life without one another.

How about you? Is your mate a part of your life to the extent that, if she or he was gone, you couldn't eat toast? On the other hand, are you and your mate engaged in helping each other grow into your true selves to such an extent that you could go on without one another?

Would you describe your partner as a healthy soulmate? Is your relationship a healthy, intimate space for soul making? Is your relationship one that perseveres through difficulty? Are you willing to work with your mate to co-create a relationship that nurtures both of your souls?

Thread 2.9

Myth: Myths are not true

Resolve: We will co-create a "true" myth to live into

Sitting above the home bar cabinet in our family room are a number of empty wine bottles. Most notably is an empty bottle of *Chateau St. Michelle*, cabernet sauvignon, that Ann and I shared with our two closest friends, Dick and Bonnie. At the time, Dick's body was ravaged with cancer and we were sharing what we thought might be our last dinner together in Seattle's Space Needle.[1] That wine has taken on mythic qualities for me, because it was also the first Washington wine we sampled when we moved to Seattle. We seldom drank Chateau St. Michelle because, at ten dollars a bottle, it was a bit steep for us in those days. For me, drinking *Chateau St. Michelle's* cabernet sauvignon, has come to represent quality, doing something special and out of the ordinary, and wonderful moments of connection. Are these three elements always present when I share a bottle of the Chateau's cab? Certainly not. But that does not make all that it represents any less true.

Another empty bottle sitting above the bar is labeled, *True Myth*, a Paso Robles wine from True Myth Wineries. When I first saw this wine in a local store, I wasn't able to buy it. Then, a couple weeks later my brother-in-law and his wife served us *True Myth* during dinner at their house. I immediately asked if I could take the bottle. They were

---

1 Dick's body finally gave out two months later.

reasonably curious as to my attraction to this wine label. "Well," I explained, "in opposition to common beliefs about myth, I think myths are inherently true."

We have just engaged eight threads of conversation about common myths. Whereas, most people associate the idea of myth with that which is not true, myths exist because they always hold some truth that helps us explain our view of reality. Think back to the threads about gender and sex and losing yourself. All of the myths we discussed in association with these topics have something true about them or they would have no staying power.

Of primary interest to me is how myths function to help represent and maintain an ideology—what is true—for a particular individual, relationship, or group. Myths create and maintain meaning through narratives that serve as explanatory frameworks for how the world works. These frameworks guide us in determining what we should deem as meaningful and important and, subsequently, influences the choices we "should" make. Let's take a look at how we might use this process to our relational advantage.

Living into the Myth

The idea of myth can be intentionally used to strengthen our connection with others. In my book, *Just Relationships*,[2] I discuss how each of us creates a relationship frame through which we view our relationships and relationship partners. This frame influences how we interpret relational behavior (both ours and our partners') and make choices in the relationship.

Attribution theorists recognize the impact of this process when they discuss *distress maintaining* and *relationship enhancing* patterns in relationships.[3] Distress-maintaining patterns occur when partners make internal, stable attributions about the cause of their partner's "bad" behavior. A simple example would be that I create a narrative that your bad actions are a result of you being a bad person and, as such, you are unlikely to change. This narrative, whether true or not, has become for me a relational myth because it explains my relationship circumstances. It is distress-maintaining because it reinforces my hopelessness and, as such, influences my actions. I may find myself avoiding or verbally attacking my partner because I believe there is no hope for real change.

---

2 Douglas L. Kelley, *Just Relationships: Living Out Social Justice as Mentor, Family, Friend, and Lover* (New York: Routledge, 2017).

3 Valerie Manusov and Brian H. Spitzberg, "Attributes of Attribution Theory: Finding Good Cause in the Search for Theory," in *Engaging Theories in Interpersonal Communication: Multiple Perspectives*, eds. Dawn O. Braithwaite and Leslie A. Baxter (Thousand Oaks, CA: SAGE, 2008): 37–49.

In contrast, relationship-enhancing patterns recognize the impact of outside influences and our ability to respond and adapt to our environment. To return to the previous example, in this case I create a narrative that your bad actions are the result of circumstances (you've been stressed out lately), not your true self. I believe (hope) that the bad behavior is not how you really want to act and that you will choose to act differently in the future. Again, I have created a narrative, whether true or not, that has become for me a relational myth because it explains my current relational circumstances. It is relationship enhancing because it reinforces my hope that things will change and creates a reason to respond to you in a constructive manner. Rather than avoiding or attacking you for the bad behavior, I may choose to engage you in a discussion or be willing to hear your apology.

To get perspective on how these processes can work, consider what is likely to happen if Ann attributes my less-than-patient tone of voice to my personality, essentially viewing it as part of who I am and unlikely to change. This perspective is distress-maintaining because it gives us few other options other than exiting the relationship or putting up with bad behavior—nothing is going to change. On the other hand, if Ann attributes my impatient tone of voice to my family of origin and remembers that it only occurs occasionally when I'm under stress (which is true, btw!), her take on things becomes relationship enhancing because it gives us hope for changing this behavior over time ("I know you don't mean to sound impatient with me. Can we find a way to help you speak more patiently when you are stressed?").

Now, let's use a mythic lens to see how we can proactively encourage relationship enhancing perspectives and behaviors. Remember that myth-making is a means of creating and maintaining meaning through the creation of story. Whether or not the story is factual, if our identity becomes tied to the story, we will begin living in a way that is consistent with what we hope to be our *true myth*. That means that we can build our relationships around relationship-enhancing myths as a means of creating and maintaining intimacy in our relationships.

Research by a number of relationship scholars has demonstrated this very effect.[4] For instance, communication scholars Rachel Reznik, Michael Roloff, and Courtney Waite Miller report that couples who take a soulmate[5] approach to their relationships "put a positive frame on relationship problems, which allows people who want to confront their partners to avoid

---

4 Thomas N. Bradbury and Frank D. Fincham, "Attributions and Behavior in Marital Interaction," *Journal of Personality and Social Psychology* 63, no. 4 (1992): 613–28, http://dx.doi.org/10.1037/0022-3514.63.4.613.

5 See the previous thread in this conversation for more on soulmates.

maladaptive sequences."[6] Further, they suggest that holding these positive illusions about the relationship may prompt relational partners to respond to minor and moderate threats positively, with affection. In essence, couples who hold a healthy perspective on being soulmates may live into their relationship myth. By believing their relationship is "meant to be" they may actually engage in prosocial behaviors consistent with that belief and that will help maintain the relationship.

Growing Close 2.9.1

Could you and one of your relationship partners create a relationship myth that would benefit your relationship? That might sound a bit challenging, but it's something you are likely already doing.

For instance, Ann and I have a wall in our breakfast room that is covered with framed photos of family and special places. To get on the wall a picture needs to have the right balance of color, but more importantly it needs to be family or showcase special moments from our travels. Do our lives always look like these pictures? Of course not.[7] But, these pictures create a myth that we live into—as family (or a couple) we travel, experience new things, and often have fun together. What are the myths you would like to live into with those you care for and love?

---

6 Rachel M. Reznik, Michael E. Roloff, and Courtney Waite Miller, "There Is Nothing as Calming as a Good Theory: How a Soulmate Theory Helps Individuals Experience Less Demand/Withdraw and Stress" in *Communicating Interpersonal Conflict in Close Relationships*, ed. Jennifer A. Samp (New York: Routledge, 2016), 44.

7 By the way, a potential negative outcome of living into your myth is if you create a myth that doesn't have much truth in it and then find yourself suffering when reality hits. For example, it could lead to significant family conflict if Ann and I view our family myth as "we are fun," yet that's not how our children have typically experienced family life. Also, take care when creating "myths" and observing others' myths on social media (for example, all of our happy pictures on Facebook). These can have a variety of social psychological effects, both positive and negative (see Paul Best, Roger Manktelow, and Brian Taylor, "Online Communication, Social Media and Adolescent Wellbeing: A Systematic Narrative Review," *Children and Youth Services Review* 41, (2014): 27–36, https://doi.org/10.1016/j.childyouth.2014.03.001; Junghyun Kim and Jong-Eun Roselyn Lee, "Facebook Paths to Happiness: Effects of the number of Facebook Friends and Self Presentation on Subjective Well-being," *Cyberpsychology Behavior and Social Networking* 14, 359–364, DOI:10.1089/cyber.2010.0374

Intimate Reflections

Every four to six weeks I get together with Ron in his living room to sing folk songs and play guitar. A few months back, when at a car show together, we each got free t-shirts with the words, *Hell Cats*, on the front. We immediately began joking that this could be the name and uniform of our "band." We've never played publicly together, but we've compiled a "set" that would take 30–40 minutes to play—if we ever get up the nerve to perform at an open mic bar or manage to get a gig.

Are we a band? Hard to tell. But we are currently living into this "band" myth and it is helping to sustain our music and our friendship.[8] The key is that our music-based, relational mythology is helping to create and sustain our intimate experience as friends.

We began this thread discussing the intimate experience that is often created when I share Chateau St. Michelle's cabernet sauvignon with family and friends. It is good wine, especially at that price, but as far as I know they don't add relationship magic to the mix as they bottle each harvest. The relationship magic is a myth, one that I am often able to live into when I share a glass with others. Because of my personal history, *Chateau St. Michelle* wine triggers a relational frame for me that makes intimate experience with others more likely.

It is with this in mind that we turn attention to *Conversation Three: Experiencing Intimacy: Connecting and Becoming.* Here I share stories and anecdotes from the *IPR* study to help us better understand how we might live into the *true myth of intimacy* through talk, sex, play, conflict, grief, and forgiveness.

---

8 Maybe by the time this book is published you'll be able to find us on a Friday night in the back of a small pizza joint in Phoenix!

Conversation Three

Experiencing Intimacy:
Connecting and Becoming

Thread 3.1

Intimate Moments

This final conversation offers fresh perspectives as to how we can experience intimate moments. Here I share stories and anecdotes that individuals shared with me during their participation in the *IPR* study. The purpose of this study was to explore peoples' experience of intimacy, specifically across six different contexts: talk, sex, play, grief, conflict, and forgiveness. As I hope you have embraced through our first two conversations, intimacy occurs in all kinds of relationships and certainly is more than simply having sex. In fact, having lost a friend and two family members to cancer, six years ago, I can hardly think of times more intimate than the interactions surrounding those events.

There is no attempt here to claim that the intimacy themes described by our respondents are comprehensive. Undoubtably, across communities and continents, there are varied experiences beyond what I report here. I am also not suggesting that your intimacy experience should be modeled after those of the *IPR* respondents. However, I hope the examples and themes offered in the following threads will encourage you to continue to explore intimacy in your relational world. And, I'm certain you will find plenty of challenges and opportunities to rethink how you are doing intimacy or, perhaps better stated, being intimate.

The following conversational threads focus on peoples' experience of intimacy through talk, sex, play, grief, conflict, and forgiveness. To get at this information, in six separate questions, I asked our participants to:

Please describe a time where _____ (talking, play, sex, grieving, conflict, forgiveness) has demonstrated or created intimacy in one of your relationships.

Once we had our participants' responses we analyzed them through a process that went something like this—my research team (three graduate students and myself) individually read through the anecdotes and stories of each context (talk, sex, play, etc.) looking for themes related to intimacy. We then came together in a college classroom and my three research assistants, across multiple white boards, wrote the themes that had emerged for each of them as they individually read the participants' offerings. Each in turn described the themes they had written, and I followed up by asking questions for clarification. I initially took a backseat in this process because I had my own ideas about intimacy that had been formulated over twenty plus years of teaching and writing (you read about these in the *Introduction* and *Conversation One*). My job at this point was to glean fresh insight by listening to what the participants had written and what my research assistants had seen. We, then, through a process of comparing and contrasting themes that each of us had seen in the data, whittled down one set of themes for each context (talking, play, sex, grieving, conflict, forgiveness). Finally, one of my graduate assistants, Hannah, put the themes in final form, and she and I had multiple conversations about terms and phrases that would ultimately be used to describe our participants' intimacy experience. We worked extremely hard to make certain that these final themes best reflect the language that our participants used.

In as much as I use participant language to describe participant themes, I also frame these findings in terms of the intimacy model we discussed in *Thread 1.4*. As a reminder, *the Model of Intimate Relating: The Process of Discovery and Connection (MIR, Model of Intimate Relating)* frames intimacy as a process of discovery and connection. We discover one another in our intimate spaces informationally, socially, physically, and psychologically (including our emotional experience). And it is the feelings of connection during this discovery that complete the intimate experience. These feelings can be a positive, joyous experience, sensing that you are understood by another human being, or sad and heart-wrenching, as long as they leave you feeling more connected to the other person.

Intimate Reflections

One of the joys of conducting this type of research is that you are never quite sure what you are going to discover. My research team and I spent hundreds of hours working through the generous narratives provided by our research participants and I want to take time to discuss one element that surprised me. It is not represented as a theme in our analysis, yet stood out again and again—it is the idea of *moments*. During one of our early sessions, Mary, a graduate student who managed the IPR study, was the first to frame our participants' responses this way—people were essentially describing for us their moments of intimacy.

What is so provocative about the idea of *moment*? Let's consider three aspects of what it means to experience an intimate moment with another human being. First, participants in the IPR study described intimate moments in ways closely associated with the characteristics of mindfulness. When asked about what intimacy means, one participant told us, "Being fully attentive to another person exclusively for a moment of time is how I view it." You will see this theme surface time and again in the following threads—one has to be present, to relationally show up, in order to experience intimacy. Aware, attentive, no judgment. A safe space where good things can happen.

Second, experiencing safe space allows for intimate moments characterized by reciprocal sharing. One experiences relational safety when there is trust, loyalty, and a sense of being understood by the other. As one participant put it:

> *Being intimate requires being closely connected. Sharing stories, experiences, details, that are personal, sensitive, emotional. There is a high level of trust, loyalty and understanding.*

And, this reciprocal sharing is not limited to our use of words:

> *We also share intimate moments by cuddling/holding each other, scratching each other's backs/massaging, and playing with each other's hair.*

One woman told as that, simply put,

> *Intimacy means sharing yourself with another person.*

Finally, our respondents conveyed that intimate moments are meaningful. They are experienced as unique or special in some way—

Intimacy to me means sexual affection and it means a deep, raw, and real relationship ... meaningful moments and talks create intimacy for me.

Similarly, other respondents described intimate moments as "special" and even "sacred." I particularly like the word "sacred" because sacred can be understood as describing something that is set apart from the norm— something unique and extraordinary is happening here.

I am happy to report that as a research team, we experienced intimate moments, as well. Our discussion, and constant comparing of perspectives and terms we used to describe the data,[1] were wonderfully stimulating, mindful times—fully present and aware of one another, asking questions and sharing without judgment. These times were safe spaces where we reciprocally shared our views and our own experiences as reference points to try and understand the data. And, yes, the times were deeply meaningful, almost sacred. As one research assistant, Darbie, later shared, "Thank you so much for allowing me to be a part of this project. It really is an honor and privilege to be able to see into so many people's lives, minds and experiences. I love this work." This sentiment was true for us all.

As we encounter our participants' stories and anecdotes in the next few threads, let's approach these offerings with mindful presence and reciprocal sharing (you'll have time to reflect on your own experience during each thread), with awareness that we are sharing in something that is deeply meaningful, distinctly set apart.

---

1 For a good discussion of the constant comparative method see Sarah J. Tracy, *Qualitative Research Methods: Collecting Evidence, Crafting Analysis, Communicating Impact* (West Sussex, England: John Wiley & Sons, 2013).

Thread 3.2

Intimacy
Through Talk

My wife, Ann, and I had been dating for two years when she decided to attend Westmont College, in Santa Barbara, CA, leaving me behind in Phoenix. It only took one semester before she had dumped me, started dating another man, and was in short time engaged. She and I continued to talk by phone weekly (in the days of land lines attached to the wall and high long-distance costs) during this time. Needless to say, the engagement eventually ended and we have currently been married 39 years. Over the years I have often heard her reflect, "During that time at Westmont, I should have realized that I could still talk to you in a way that I couldn't talk to my fiancé."

Talk in many peoples' experience forms the foundation of intimacy. As we discussed in the opening conversation of this book, talk is a central way we discover one another's intimate spaces. Before we launch into this section, let's remember that every person is unique and values different ways of experiencing intimacy. As in all of the following threads, the examples shared here are not intended to be a prescription for intimacy, but rather an encouragement to what you might already be practicing and a catalyst for exploring talk in your relationships in new ways. So let's take a look at how people in the *IPR*[1] of experiencing discovery and connection with those for whom they care.

Talk as the Way to Intimacy

> *Talking is the way to being intimate … If you don't talk about things, how do you plan on building a relationship where you bond and find something intimate?*

So offered one of our female respondents. And in case you're tempted to think this is primarily a female perspective, one of our male respondents put it just as clearly:

> *Talking and getting to know the person is always the basis.*

On the flip side, the importance of talk becomes most evident when it is difficult to share verbally with your partner. Listen to the plight of one young man:

> *Well in my last relationship I had a hard time expressing how I really feel about her, and I swear on everything I loved her in my heart. I was going through a hard time in life at the time and was overwhelmed. I messed up and wasn't sharing my life with her, but she was sharing hers with me. But talking is everything in a relationship because if you don't know what your partner's needs are, how are you both going to grow together and take your relationship to the next level of life?*

This recounting poignantly illustrates the necessity for intimate moments to be based on reciprocal sharing[2]: "I messed up and wasn't sharing my life with her, but she was sharing hers with me." The challenge of using talk to create and express intimacy is that, at times, we are hurting, tired, or distraught and the words simply don't come easily.

Another key aspect of words, brought out in the previous quote, is *knowing* your partner: "if you don't know what your partner's needs are, how are you both going to grow together and take your relationship to the next level of life." In fact, "to know" or "knowing" were frequently mentioned

---

1 *IPR*, Intimacy in Personal Relationships study.
2 Note that reciprocal sharing is one of the key elements of creating intimate moments. For more on this, see *Thread 1.3*.

Growing Close 3.2.1

Reciprocity and sharing are essential elements of intimacy. In long-term relationships, reciprocity is often across interactions, rather during a single interaction. For instance, at this moment, my wife is ill, and the last thing she needs is reciprocity. She just needs me to listen to how she feels and make her another cup of tea. Yet, when the tables are turned, such that I'm not feeling well, she will be ready for reciprocity and serve me well.

If reciprocal sharing can be difficult for you, try talking about it with your partner when times are good. You might say something like, "You know that when I'm stressed it's hard for me to talk. It's okay to ask me questions, but it would help if you would give me time to be ready to share."

by *IPR* participants. As we explored in *Conversation One,* there is something powerful in being known, discovered by another human being and still accepted (remember our previous hide and seek discussion?). This, of course, is a central aspect of the *Model of Intimate Relating* (MIR),[3] which describes intimacy as a process of discovery and connection. So let's take a look at how these ideas emerge in *what* we talk about.

What We Talk About

To more fully understand how we discover one another it's helpful to think about *what* it is we are discovering. *IPR* participants told us that the nature of intimate talk is varied, consisting of everything from complimenting one another to sharing deep secrets, and that often the deeper elements were difficult to share or had often never been shared with anyone else. Deep sharing can also consist of more positive information focusing on the future and, most intriguing, to me, we discovered that a number of people used the word "truth" to describe what was shared. Let's take a closer look these elements.

---

3 *The Model of Intimate Relating: The Process of Discovery and Connection.* For more on this, see the previous thread.

A common way people develop intimacy through talk is to reveal something about oneself that no one else (or few others) knows. As noted by one of our participants, these intimate moments can take on a meaningful, even sacred character:

> *I have had various times where talking has been intimate due to what we were talking about. It was kind of sacred and enclosed secretly. The other person trusted me with the information they were telling me.*

Trust is often a precondition and a byproduct of this kind of sharing providing a safe space to build connection:

> *An example of a time in which talking has demonstrated intimacy was when my husband confided in me and told me secrets that he had never shared with anyone else. It made our connection and bond stronger and brought us closer to one another.*

People also told us that they talk about their shared experiences and dream about the future. For instance, we heard about sisters and romantic partners who were drawn together by talking about their childhood, a mom and daughter who felt closer after discussing their common "personal challenges," and friends who were drawn together after discovering they had a shared experience of feeling rejected. Others told us that talking about the future and jointly planning for it enhanced their intimate experience with their partners.

A final element our *IPR* folks talked about surprised me when I first saw it—truth. People described this "intimate truth" in various ways. One participant stated:

> *[accepting the] truth (though exaggerated) of the views we expressed in the heat of the fight.*

In this particular relationship, although exaggerated things were said during the heat of battle, they were able to realize the hard truth embedded within the exaggeration of what was said, as well as the trust they had for one another to be able to work through such a difficult process. This actually helped them grow closer to one another.

Another aspect of truth was described as follows:

> *Knowing deep truths about someone creates intimacy—knowing their history helps you know them better.*

Deep truths about someone. In *Thread 1.8* we discussed transformation that comes from finding your true self. And in *Thread 2.3* we unpacked the idea that you don't lose yourself in intimacy, you actually can find your *self*. You'll see this theme pop up throughout our participants' responses. Finding who you are comes in part from being with others who can see your "truth," and accept you for who you are.

Growing Close 3.2.2

Sharing *truth* is tricky business. What is true for you (you think you are deeply sensitive and responsive to other people) may not be true for me (I think you are way too sensitive and get prematurely involved in other peoples' business). Plus, how we deliver the "truth" makes a big difference in how we hear each other during our interactions. We explore *how we talk* in the next sections on discovery and connection, but before we do, take a minute to think about how words may or may not have been used in your relationships to know the *truth* of the other person. Here, I'm referring to those times when we discover something true about who another person is or who we are ourselves.

Recently, Ann and I were on an eight-day river rafting trip down the Grand Canyon. Coming back from a long hike I was talking with one of our river rafting guides who was interested in the fact that I teach about relationships. She told me, "I'm wanting to be much more intentional about the way I do relationships," and as we walked single file down a narrow canyon trail we talked for thirty minutes about what that might mean. Approaching camp, I turned to her and said, "Thank you for sharing. I need to hear other peoples' stories. And, your story is a beautiful one to tell." The response in her eyes told me, that in that moment, she had learned something true about herself—*my story is beautiful*! And I had been reminded of a truth, too—*it is beautiful when I listen*.

Talk as Discovery

Individuals' rich descriptions of experiencing intimate talk highlight the importance of creating a safe space for discovering one another. In *Thread 1.6* we explored the idea of vulnerability along with fear and risk and the need to develop trust. It's hard to be discovered if you're unwilling to be vulnerable. Our respondents echoed these themes:

> I was going through an emotionally hard time in my life and became really depressed because I was unsure of where my future was headed. I began to explain to my boyfriend my anxieties and why I was unhappy with life. I started to cry and he pulled me close to him and held me while I cried. I felt very vulnerable and it created a different kind of intimacy between us.

As this quote beautifully illustrates, people are willing to talk intimately when they feel safe. Another *IPR* respondent brought this out more explicitly:

> A time where talking has demonstrated intimacy is when I felt safe and loved enough to be able to open up about a past experience that has altered my life that I do not share with everyone.

Clearly for these individuals feeling vulnerable yet safe is essential to intimacy. Though, for many, feeling safe goes beyond simply knowing your partner will keep your secret "safe." A central aspect of feeling safe and trusting others is sensing that they understand you. If you don't think someone truly "gets" you, understands how you think and feel, you remain uncertain as to whether they may inadvertently hurt you. Consider the following:

> It was very hard for me to be honest with my then-boyfriend (now spouse) about some of the situations I experienced in my childhood. I wanted him to understand why I was who I was, and why I felt so strongly about certain things inside a relationship. It was our first "serious" conversation, and he shared some things, too. It created a stronger bond between us.

This articulate statement regarding understanding emphasizes the desire to be discovered, understood, in terms of why we are the way we are. She wants to know that he "gets" her. Importantly, she also notes that this desire for sharing and understanding was mutual. Participants frequently suggested that intimate moments are characterized by mutual understanding, free of judgment:

> *Talking about moments in life that are hard to talk about but have shaped you. It's a mutual understanding that you will not be judged, but rather understood.*

Talk as Connection

As we have seen, discovery through talk is characterized by vulnerability, safety, and mutual understanding, and facilitates a sense of connection. Common in *IPR* responses was the preposition "with." People told us that they "shared with" their partners. Consistent with our earlier discussion of treating others as persons,[4] our respondents recognized the importance of speaking *with* others, rather than speaking *at* them.

Share is another interesting word that reflects how we do intimate talk. To share implies the giving of something you own. It can be an invitation to co-own something with someone you trust.[5] In this sense, sharing one's secrets, hurts, embarrassments, mistakes, dreams, hopes, and fears builds a deep sense of discovery and connection.

As you might guess, a number of our participants described using their words to "share with" their partners. And, people described connecting by using words to help, support, comfort, affirm, and show gratitude. Of course, people also talked about listening—the critical ability to receive and understand the words of our partners. And, a significant means of demonstrating and building connection. The following quote from one of our participants pulls together a number of these themes as they describe creating a sense of closeness. We should all be so lucky as to have such a friend!

> *I was able to share with a friend my true feelings about my life, my relationships, my failures and my future fears. I trusted this person immensely. I knew they loved me unconditionally and without judgement. I knew the things I shared would NEVER be used against me or to hurt me. I knew they would listen and comfort me. This is a closeness I've never been able to duplicate, anywhere or with anyone else.*

---

4 See *Thread 1.1.*
5 See *Thread 1.3* for more on privacy, intimacy, and co-owning.

Growing Close 3.2.3

When one of my aunts, whom I dearly loved, would call on the phone, my dad would call out to my mom, "Shirley, Sandra wants to talk at you!" And that's the way it was. And, for one of my friends, his mom would call him, report a number of things on her mind, then say, "It was good to catch up," and hang up. When my friend was fast enough he would catch her before she tapped "end call," so that he could reciprocally share.

Both relationships in the preceding examples where limited by one partner not letting the other participate—they represent *at* relational approaches, rather than *with*. Do you *share with* those you care for? Do you give support, comfort, help, or thanks? Do you have relationships where you feel safe enough to express your feelings about your partner or your own life experience (your fears, hopes, frustrations, dreams)? Honestly, do you *share with* or mostly *talk at* those you love?

Connection is also demonstrated by spending *time* with others. This important relational message (you are important enough to spend time with) is inherent in all of the contexts we will discuss in this conversation (talk, sex, play, grief, conflict, forgiveness). Our respondents frequently noted the importance of spending time together talking, and even losing track of time, regardless of whether the topics were specifically deep or simply a casual means of connection. In my book, *Marital Communication*, I argue that, while the bricks of the house are essential (the deep meaningful conversations), it is the common everyday talk that is the mortar connecting the bricks.[6] Listen to this quote from a dating couple illustrating the use of "meaningless conversations" as the mortar in their relationship:

---

6 Douglas L. Kelley, *Marital Communication*, (Cambridge, England: Polity Press, 2012).

My girlfriend and I have amazing talks just laying on the couch Sundays. Most of the time they are meaningless conversations but it brings us so much closer.

And of course respondents told us that carving out time for deep talks (the bricks) was also used to maintain connection:

When a friend and I began to date our intimacy grew since after a week of dating he had to return to school in Berkeley. Not being able to be together beyond text messages and FaceTime calls, we grew intimate by talking deeply though the late hours of many summer nights.

Intimate Reflections

Intimate talk is revealing, co-owned, shared, expressive, and caring. It is associated with feeling safe enough to be vulnerable, trusting another person to understand you. Intimate talking sends a message that you and your partner are worth it!

And, while, for some individuals, intimacy is synonymous with talk, others associate intimacy with sex, and still others recognize the strong connection between the two. In fact, a number of respondents noted that intimate talk often leads to affectionate touch, including sex:

Very private conversations and feeling extra comfortable created one thing that led to the other in a more sexual way.

So let's turn to the next thread of conversation and discover how sex can become a beautifully intimate relational space.

Thread 3.3

Intimacy Through Sex

ntimacy and sex have a long, complicated history together. Sex has started wars, destroyed relationships, been viewed as a commodity, and used to establish status and control others (#metoo). Nonetheless, sex continues to play a significant role in personal relationships. One powerful aspect of sex is that it has the potential to tap into all four of the intimate spaces we identified in *MIR*[1] (information, social, physical, and psychological/emotional).

Our focus in this thread of conversation is on the intimate experience of sex. What is it that makes the difference between sex that is self-centered, controlling, or just for sport and that which is experienced as intimacy?

IPR participants provided a variety of takes regarding sex and intimacy. A few *IPR* participants, when asked to "describe what intimacy means to you," equated sex with intimacy:

Being sexually involved with another person.

---

1 Just a reminder that *MIR* is the *Model of Intimate Relating* and focuses on discovery and connection. Discovery takes place across four intimate spaces (information, social, physical, and psychological/emotional).

and,

Sharing sexual desires with others.

Yet, as we discussed in *Conversation Two*, it is clear that not all sex is intimate. Many participants reflected this understanding in their responses. They discussed sex in ways that recognized the discovery and connection aspects of intimacy, along with intimate qualities such as vulnerability, trust, and being mindfully present. We'll spend most of the forthcoming discussion on these issues. But, responses to the *IPR* survey also focused on foundational perspectives as to the connection between sex and intimacy and the potential relational and personal outcomes and functions of sex, so let's start there.

Perspectives and Outcomes

As you might guess, people's perspectives on sex and intimacy vary widely. Some *IPR* respondents told us that sex was not necessary for intimacy,

I don't think sex (penetration) is necessary in a relationship

while others purported that sex was essential:

Sex is crucial in a relationship,

and,

If you're not having mind blowing sex with your partner than you're missing out!

Some viewed intimate sex as a sign of exclusivity that "seals the relationship," in a way that is special,

The first time I had sex with this person we became so much closer on a relational level due to the fact that we don't just do that with anybody and it was something special.

and worth waiting for,

> *When I met my boyfriend he was at the beginning stages of a divorce. We both agreed to not kiss or have sex until the divorce was finalized. Waiting until that day made it extra special because we had been waiting so long to express our intimacy towards one another.*

while for others ...

> *Sex in my relationships has never deepened or created intimacy. It's just been gritty, pulling gravel from my knees sex.*

SEX WITHOUT INTIMACY

To this last point, it's important to recognize that not all adults have had sex or an intimate experience with sex. In fact, some of our respondents told us they didn't respond to our question because it made them uncomfortable[2] or because they had never had sex. On the flip side there were those (as in the previous quote) who reported having sex, but never experiencing intimacy with sex. The reasons for not experiencing intimacy varied considerably. Some persons were simply not interested in building intimacy through their sexual experience, while others avoided intimacy because of negative past experiences. All of these individuals, for one reason or another, positive or negative, were not interested in developing the relationship beyond the physical aspect. One person simply stated their intentional disconnect between intimacy and sex:

> *Never, I leave shortly after.*

Another seemed a bit confused that the intimate physical connection had never turned into emotional or psychological closeness:

> *Well, I am currently in an "intimate" relationship with someone I have never been "intimate" with. It's interesting because we have extremely passionate sex but we never get deep in conversation. There are times we have sex and the sex is so intense it feels like there are feelings involved. But there is not. It's a weird situation.*

For others, the lack of emotional connection had been a choice based on past experience,

---

2 For each context (talk, sex, and so on), I gave participants options to respond if the question did not apply or make sense to them.

> *Personally for me, because I have never been in a long term relationship sex has not created or demonstrated intimacy for me very often. I learned early on not to get deep feelings for a man if the relationship is strictly sexual.*

or, tragically, due to patterns of negative sexual experiences:

> *I have a really negative history with sex. My first partner was sexually abusive (I was 18) and I was raped my first year of college (I was 19, I think, maybe 20). Because of this, I have a very difficult time experiencing sex positively. I've found that in all of my relationships, sex has led to a decrease in intimacy over time, through violation of trust, and unaligned expectations.*

SEX WITH INTIMACY

In sharp contrast to the experiences reported above, the majority of our respondents reported experiencing intimate moments that led to sex,

> *Sex can definitely create intimacy, but sex or making love is most powerful after an intimate moment has led to the sex itself.*

or sex that was surprisingly experienced as intimacy,

> *Engaging in sex with eyes open and focused on my lover's from initiation until after orgasm provided a surprising emotional experience that can only be described as "intimate" ******.*

or a deepening of intimacy:

> *Sex is obviously something intimate all on its own, in my opinion. But i had sex with my boyfriend for the first time last week, and he was constantly checking on me. He kept asking if what he was doing was okay, if i needed anything. He just made things really comfortable and therefore i think more intimate. He makes me feel more like myself.*

For our respondents who primarily experienced intimacy with sex, the following statement, sums it up:

> *There is an undeniable bond. When you are holding one another. Kissing, hugging, loving on each other. There is a unity. Physical touch is powerful.*

> ## Growing Close 3.3.1
>
> How intentional have you been about the role of sex in your relationships? Perhaps it sounds a bit clinical, but if you are sexually active, take a moment to think about the sexual outcomes you've experienced regarding intimacy. Have they been mostly positive or negative? How has your experience or perspective on sex changed over time? Would you like to consider ways to develop intimacy once sex has become part of your relationships? If you are not sexually active, consider these same questions and your relational goals for intimacy.
>
> One of our respondents told us how she and her partner intentionally change their sexual routine to facilitate intimacy:
>
> > *Every now and again my partner and i will slow down our time together. Slowing down and enjoying that time has created and strengthened our intimacy.*
>
> If you are stuck for ideas on how to do this in your relationship, read on, because *IPR* respondents gave us plenty of ideas as to how intimate sex looks and feels.

Intimate Sex

One thing my research team and I learned as we read about relational partners' intimate experiences is that intimate sex occurs at a variety of times and fulfills a variety of functions in the relationship. Five types of intimate sex stood out to us: sex after time apart, make-up sex, sex as comfort, sex as a shared and pleasurable activity, and sex as "soul tie." One function of intimate sex is to help partners reconnect after physically being apart from one another,

We almost broke up once. I came back from a long trip and she was so unhappy from not seeing me in so long. We talked for hours, not a fight, just a talk. We worked out all the negative emotions we had been holding in and she finally let out how frustrated she was that I was gone for so long. We worked it out and after that ... well ya know. It was one of the closest times I have ever felt with her and after that our relationship has been so much stronger.

or being apart because of "taking a break" from the relationship:

My boyfriend and I were going through a very tough time in our relationship. It got to the point where we took a break, which involved no communication at all and not seeing each other. But there were at least two days that I can remember where we broke those rules. I would go over to his house late at night and we would have sex. It was "I miss you" make-up sex, and it was some of the best sex we had up to that point. It definitely confirmed that we still wanted to be with each other and created a new form of intimacy and closeness that we needed at that time in our relationship.

In both of these cases, sex was used to reaffirm the relationship, to reestablish a commitment to one another. Related, *IPR* participants reported that intimate sex was used to increase the level of comfort in the relationship. In fact, the importance of being comfortable with one another during intimate sex was mentioned quite frequently by *IPR* respondents:[3]

Couples grow closer when they share a bed and also their bodies. Sexual interaction with my partner has made our relationship more comfortable and now we believe in a physical connection rather than just an emotional one.

Of course, people also talked about intimate sex as doing something together that feels good. These "feel good" moments are provided by one's partner and, as such, the shared altruism (mutually helping one another feel good) becomes a significant source of connection:

You are also making your partner feel good which reinforces the feeling of togetherness

---

3 When we started the *IPR* study I was aware that being comfortable with your partner is a sign of intimacy, but I wouldn't have predicted that it would be mentioned frequently by participants. As you will see in the upcoming threads, being comfortable with friends, family members, and lovers is a prominent characteristic of being intimate.

IPR participants also described connection as emerging from an experi-ence of vulnerability and trust between partners that feels special or sacred. Consider the following quote wherein a young woman recognizes the comfort that can come with sex, but also the vulnerability inherent to discovery ("to let you see me at my most vulnerable"). She, then, extends her description to include the deeper emotional connection, or *soul-tie*, that is created as a result of this process:

> *Sex has created a sense of trust within my relationships. It shows that I am comfortable enough with you to let you see me at my most vulnerable. Sex for me is also very emotion based. Sex is a soul tie so whenever I take that step with someone I am letting them in and giving them the chance to hurt me.*

Importantly, this rather stunning revelation frames intimate sex as a process of discovery and connection. We'll unpack this quote, later, but for now let's take a closer look at discovery and connection[4] as they emerge during sex.

Sex as Discovery

A number of themes that emerged from *IPR* stories are rooted in partners' discovery of one another. The man who provided the following quote seems almost surprised that they are still having frequent sex now that the couple is engaged. For him there seems to be a reciprocal relationship between knowing (discovery) and sex,

> *My fiancé and I still have sex frequently in our relationship and as we've grown to know each other more the sex we have is more passionate and intimate than it would be with a stranger.*

and as another participant noted discovery is mutual:[5]

> *[sex] allowed us to become connected by learning each other's desires.*

---

4 Key elements of MIR (*Model of Intimate Relating*) as discussed in the previous thread and in *Conversation One*.

5 In *Conversation One* we discussed the fact that love can be unilateral (that is, I can love you even if you don't love me), whereas intimacy is bilateral (you can share and be vulnerable, but the relationship is not intimate unless both partners engage in discovery and connection at some level).

There is something very powerful about the idea that intimacy is mutual, each partner learning about the other's likes and dislikes. Each person discovering more about the other. Intimate moments, such as these, are based in the reciprocal sharing that takes place both verbally and nonverbally between partners.

Discovery also takes place through positive uncertainty. That is, when partners feel comfortable with each other there is freedom for novelty and creativity, both of which create a positive and stimulating sense of discovery and connection. Consider the following from one of our Scorpio respondents:

> Well, I love having sex, I'm a Scorpio. I love trying new things with the partner I'm with and I want to look sexy naked for my partner. If I'm with someone, I need to be physically attracted to them and who they are as a person, and when I find someone like that, I want to have sex all the time—make it fun, do weird things in bed, etc. Yes, I feel good sex brings you closer as a "two," because you're comfortable being with that person naked.

Sex as Connection

The type of playful discovery, discussed above, "brings you closer as a 'two.'" Connection can be a beautiful outcome of sexual discovery. One *IPR* participant recognized this in positive ways with a friend:

> Sex has created intimacy with my friend. It just connects two individuals in a different way.

However, as another participant reported, friendship is tricky business when it comes to sex and connection:

> I didn't realize that me having sex with my friend would change the dynamic of our relationship because it made me feel a lot closer to him and I don't think it had the same effect on him.

As you might guess, we found that certain people associated love with the idea of sex and connection. As we discussed in *Thread 1.7*, a constituent element of full love is an emotional bond or connection:

I think sex and intimacy are kind of different because when I think of intimacy I think of love and caring for that person ... But you can have sex with someone without loving them and intimacy I think is normally when you have love for that person that you are having sex with.

and,

I wait to have sex with someone i am dating for a long period of time, because it is such a special moment. So when i do have sex it shows me that i do or i am falling in love with this person.

Growing Close 3.3.2

What would it mean for you to reframe intimate sex as a process of discovery and connection? How would it change things if sex became a process of mutual discovery? You don't have to view sex like our Scorpio friend, above, but it could be important to ask whether you are able to handle the uncertainty and risk of mutually discovering one another. Or, maybe the risk for you is more regarding the inevitable connection that comes with intimate sex. The following section in this conversational thread explores these issues. However, it can also be helpful to talk these things over with your partner, a close friend, or even a counselor. For many of us, our sexual "hang ups," our fear of discovery and connection, run deep. Yet, deciding to open yourself to discovery and connection can open new possibilities in terms of experiencing life's fullness.

Mindful Sex

Intimate sexual discovery and connection is facilitated by a number of interaction qualities that we have been associating with mindfulness over the course of our three conversations: being fully present and aware with one another in a way that feels safe (no judgment). Aspects of this type of intimate sex experience showed up in various descriptions provided by *IPR* respondents. In the following quote, being present and aware are movingly experienced as being one:

> *The feeling in sex when your bodies are completely one. Not trying to use the other for pleasure but coming together as one and wanting each other in the greatest capacity possible.*

Notable in this description is that the partners' bodies become "one," but so too their desires. Both partners want the other and, consequently, are wanted by the other. It is a profound experience to be wanted by someone. This cuts to the core of our essential human nature—made for intimacy.[6] Also, the partners aren't simply using each other for pleasure, but appreciating the moment—together. As another participant (referenced previously) shared:

> *Every now and again my partner and i will slow down our time together. Slowing down and enjoying that time has created and strengthened our intimacy.*

Whereas this couple slows down to enhance their intimate experience (possibly increasing their sense of presence with each other), another depiction of oneness was described as synchronized movement ("moved together") and, strikingly, sustained eye contact:

> *I am reminded of a time where the sustained eye contact as we moved together led to an intense feeling of oneness that differed from other very enjoyable activities. That was a moment that happened to us as a gift of intimacy.*

This woman's experience of presence and awareness with her partner is so profound that she describes it as a "gift." A gift facilitated by sustained eye contact as they moved. In this regard, I've often pondered that much of human sexual activity is face-to-face. Remember, in *Conversation Two*, regarding our discussion surrounding the myth that sex is intimacy, we resolved to make a gift to our self and our partner by "showing up" during sex. Perhaps we can do that by having the courage to engage one another, eye to eye.

---

6 For more on this, see *Thread 1.2*.

Of course there is tremendous risk being present and aware with one's partner. You are now known. And, having given access to all of your intimate spaces (informational, social, physical, psychological/emotional), your partner has opportunity to hurt you in ways that others can't. This means it is all the more paramount to build trust between partners, to not carelessly "give one's heart away," but rather *allow vulnerability within a safe relationship to create a deep sense of intimacy.* A quote I used earlier describes one way to view this process:

> *Sex has created a sense of trust within my relationships. It shows that I am comfortable enough with you to let you see me at my most vulnerable. Sex for me is also very emotion based. Sex is a soul tie so whenever I take that step with someone I am letting them in and giving them the chance to hurt me.*

When this woman states that she is, "giving them the chance to hurt me," she is referring to the fact the she knows she is vulnerable. Yet, she is not casually vulnerable with just anyone, recklessly risking emotional hurt. Rather, her vulnerability comes within a safe context with someone whom she trusts and feels comfortable.

Growing Close 3.3.3

It takes a tremendous amount of courage to be present with our partners. But, it also calls for us to be smart and intentional about how we are in relationship with others. How might choosing to be mindful with your partner encourage the experience of intimacy during sex? What if your partner felt like you "showed up" for sex? That you weren't there just to get your needs met? And, more than not judging, what if you actually expressed your desire for them ... as a person? Or, riskier, yet, can you imagine how you might feel if your partner came to you with this same mindful approach?[7]

Intimate Reflections

I personally have found this thread of the conversation to be captivating, surprising, and moving at times. I am so thankful for our respondents' insights and willingness to share their diverse experiences honestly (everything from *gritty, pulling gravel from my knees sex to sex is a soul tie*). I want to end with a few observations about one last theme that was raised by a few of our respondents—being naked. U. S. culture has, of late, latched on to the word "naked" for marketing purposes. You can buy Naked Juice, Naked Eyeshadow, and I was just given a pair of Buck Naked underwear. The word, naked, is often used to connote that something is all natural, free of contaminates, falsities (as in the naked truth) or constraints. Further, there is an implication of exposure. Nothing is hidden.

Perhaps the most famous story about nakedness comes from ancient Hebrew Scriptures in the book of Genesis. Here, Adam and Eve eat fruit that has been forbidden them by God and, "Then the eyes of both were opened, and they knew that they were naked. ..."[8] One commentator suggests that Adam and Eve's recognition of their own nakedness represents the recognition of self-consciousness.[9] Evidently, before choosing to disobey God's command, they walked freely naked with God in the garden. Yet, we learn as the story continues that their first response to being aware of their nakedness is to sew fig leaves together and make loincloths to cover themselves. One interpretation of this is that when we become conscious of our own nakedness (physical and psychological), we immediately hide what is vulnerable. However, by implication, the good news is that we can experience growth and freedom when we feel naked and safe.

Some of our *IPR* respondents expressed this very perspective. Listen as one respondent recognizes self-consciousness as being comfortable (or not) in one's "own skin":

> *I feel like being completely naked with someone you are having sex with creates so much intimacy, especially for someone who is not comfortable in their own skin. One person allows the other to be seen completely nude inside and out and creates this moment of sacredness.*

---

7 A gentle reminder on this one. In the introduction to *Intimate Spaces* I encourage you not to use this book to judge yourself or your partners. Instead, use this information to help you make choices and engage your relational partners in discussions that result in the co-creation of your intimate space. Remember, intimacy is hard work and takes time.

8 Genesis 3:7 New Revised Standard Version.

9 Agnes W. Norfleet, "Genesis Commentary," in *The Renovaré Spiritual Formation Study Bible*, ed. Richard J. Foster (San Francisco: HarperCollins, 1989).

For this respondent there is a sacred aspect to being "seen completely nude inside and out." Nothing hidden. Exposed. The following quote further expresses the vulnerability that comes from this type of exposure and even more so, the deep sense of gratefulness that can accompany being known by one's partner ... and accepted:

And to state the obvious, there is an intense form of vulnerability that is needed and granted during sex, what with being naked, the friction of skin on skin, being in very close proximity of each other's pheromones and other body odors; all involve a consent or relay acceptance, and to be accepted, is to be grateful, hence feeling intense intimacy.

Our next thread of conversation, intimacy through play, picks up on many of the themes we've just discussed. Play can feel like being naked with others—nothing hidden, exposed, vulnerable—and best takes place when we feel safe. As one person told us:

[Sex] is just like play, where you feel comfortable enough and feel close enough to want to be close to them in this way as well.

Thread 3.4

Intimacy Through Play

"I'll have to go back to the front pretty soon."

"We won't think about that until you go. You see I'm happy, darling, and we have a lovely time. I haven't been happy for a long time and when I met you perhaps I was nearly crazy. Perhaps I was crazy. But now we're happy and we love each other. Do let's please just be happy. Do you want to play?"

"Yes and come to bed."

—*A Farewell to Arms*, by Ernest Hemingway[1]

This thread of conversation may take you by surprise. Play is often associated with children or, at the very least, with not being an adult or mature or serious about life. Yet, famed anthropologist, Ashely Montagu has stated,

Play has probably been the most important factor in the evolution of social behavior among vertebrates and, as the distinguished

---

1 Ernest Hemingway, *A Farewell to Arms* (New York: Charles Scribner's Sons, 1929). A conversation between lovers, an injured soldier and his nurse.

biologist William H. Thorpe has remarked, probably also of the mental and spiritual life of humankind. [2]

Play, and activity that is engaged playfully, [3] provide an orientation to life characterized by discovery and connection. There is a sense of openness, joy, and creativity as one discovers the world of ideas, places, things, and, relationships. This openness to discovery gives opportunity to connect with the world and the persons with which one shares that world. As we see in the opening scenario from *A Farewell to Arms*, play can have a significant role in adult romantic relationships, but play can also be meaningful between parents and children, and with friends.

IPR respondents told us about intimacy and play in two streams of thought. The first regards the kinds of behaviors people used for play. The second reflects how people experienced intimacy through playful discovery and connection. Let's take a brief look at what individuals counted as play in their personal relationships, then move on to explore in greater detail their experience of play and intimacy.

Intimate Playful Behavior

The IPR research team found that play behaviors could be organized into five categories representing humor, games, shared activities, affectionate touch, and mock fighting. Not all of these classifications are exactly what you might think, so let's take a closer look at how they were used to create or maintain intimacy.

HUMOR

Humor showed up in peoples' responses as they talked about "jokes," "laughter," and "teasing." Sometimes humor was used to create daily connection. In this way, as we discussed in a previous thread on talk and intimacy, humor can serve as the mortar between the bricks:

> *Being able to be with my fiancé and be completely entertained by each other's presence alone by laughing together and having a good time goofing around. You can take a look back at the situation and think, "Wow, I love this moment."*

---

2 Ashley Montagu, *Growing Young*, 2nd ed. (Westport, CT: Bergin & Garvey, 1989), 131.
3 "Play" that is engaged competitively with only a desire for winning is substantively different than the playful qualities you'll be introduced to in this thread.

Somewhat counterintuitively, humor was also used to discuss serious topics or engage in conversations that might have otherwise been overly sensitive to discuss. The following quote beautifully illustrates how humor helps a parent and adult son talk about serious matters:

> *We were sitting in his backyard, just casually chatting about life, and finding humor in the many ways we deal similarly with life. Our mannerisms are similar, so we understand each other in a way that others do not. Our conversation was intimate in that it involved meaningful conversation, and our banter with one another was playful, even when we discussed serious topics.*

Humor was also used in a way that demonstrated co-ownership of shared perspectives.[4] We see this in the following scenario where two friends use an inside joke to cope with diversity. I find it particularly interesting how co-owning this particular joke served to regulate the relationship and return a sense of comfort between the friends:

> *My best friend and I danced together growing up. While growing up best friends of opposite genders can be difficult (as people start placing expectations of dating upon your friendship from the outside and you're both independently trying to go through puberty and everything), we had a running joke that always relieved the tension. So, any time we were feeling awkward or in a situation that otherwise might have driven us farther apart, we would go off on that joke and it broke the tension, allowing us to remain comfortable with each other despite everything else.*

GAMES

The frequent use of this theme is not surprising with the social/cultural prevalence of video games in the U.S., although participants discussed other types of game-playing, as well. Many respondents recalled times where game playing brought them closer to other participants as they worked towards the same goal. Interestingly, even opposition during game playing could facilitate intimacy. Listen in as this young woman discusses the benefits of a little friendly competition—time spent together, playfulness as her partner sees her "get worked up," comforting, and helping:

---

4 See *Thread* 1.3 for more on privacy, co-ownership, and intimacy.

"My boyfriend loves when I take time out of my day to sit down and play Mario Kart with him. He loves the time spent together, the friendly competition that comes along with racing each other. He gets joy out of seeing me get worked up when I lose and loves comforting me and giving me tips on how to be better."

SHARED ACTIVITIES

Shared activities are different from games in that that they are generally non-competitive activities. Although, like games, there is a playful quality to them as individuals are simultaneously involved in a shared space, often for enjoyment. The *IPR* respondents reported a variety of shared activities, such as "attending concerts," "dancing," and "going out and doing something fun." In a majority of circumstances, shared activities were rooted in a hobby or leisure activity belonging to one or both members of the relationship, and typically ones that individuals felt strongly connected to and wanted to share with one another. In this way, shared activities provide a window into relational partners' passions. This window is not necessarily verbal, yet, can create a sense of connection. The following quote demonstrates how one of our *IPR* women found a way to stay connected to her active father:

My dad and I do Spartan races together and do Crossfit together, and it helps us feel closer to each other.

AFFECTIONATE TOUCH

The affectionate touch category includes all physical contact that is deemed as caring or nurturing. Many described this type of physical connection as a means of demonstrating presence, support, and comfort. Importantly, affectionate touch often created a shared experience of the moment. Affectionate touch was often portrayed as transformative in that it took ordinary moments, such as cooking dinner, and created a space where intimacy could flourish. The following quote provides a good example of just such a moment:

We love riding on the back of his motorcycle. He is relaxed, I am relaxed, we have physical contact, but we don't (can't) really talk to each other. When we come to a red light, he will reach his hand back and hold my calf for a few seconds and I squeeze his arm.

MOCK FIGHTING

Mock fighting was described using words and phrases, such as, "wrestling," "play fighting," and "tickling." This type of play is typically physical and usually occurs for an extended period of time. Essential to mock fighting is having permission to "invade" a partner's personal space and knowing how long to remain there.

I remember wrestling with my younger son when he was about four-years old. I was over him, looking down at him, when he began to panic because it was evening and he wasn't used to seeing me in the dim light with my newly sprouted beard. I immediately stopped, asked him if he was okay, and asked him if he wanted me to shave my beard. He told, "I'm okay and I like the beard. I just freaked out. Let's keep wrestling!"

A 45-year-old female respondent described a similar mock fighting moment with an adult friend. Here we see mock fighting's close relationship to affectionate touch and being mindfully present with one's partner:[5]

I remember vividly joking and even physically playing around, wrestling with a man I cared very much about … All of a sudden he had me pinned and was hovering over me. We were gazing into each other's eyes. It was silent for what felt like endless minutes. We both somehow looked into each other's souls and saw a need to be loved and saw fear of rejection and uncertainty but we kissed and it was a beautiful tender time where we were able to fill an aching void in each other's heart.

This powerful description provides a picture of mock fighting that can serve as a safe entry point to truly affectionate touch and mindful intimacy. Clearly the couple in this scenario found themselves present with each other, aware, and fully accepted—filling the "aching void" we all deal with, at times, in our lives.

Growing Close 3.4.1

Where would you place yourself on the play spectrum? If you don't consider yourself a playful person, consider rethinking the nature of play. People in our study reported play as everything from games to wrestling to going to the symphony.

---

5 It is important, to recognize that whereas mock fighting represents a healthy connection between partners, this type of behavior can morph into control by one partner if appropriate boundaries are not expressed and respected.

Ashley Montagu considers imagination to be play—playing with ideas. Me too. I consider my writing and teaching to be play. I want these creative endeavors to be useful to others, but there are parts of them that I engage simply because I enjoy doing it. It's fun and stimulating, in a broad sense of those words, rather like running a marathon is fun for some people. What's fun and stimulating to you? Can you intentionally introduce these types of play into your relationships?

Years ago when my youngest son, Daniel, was about five years old, he and Ann played the rhyming hand-clapping game, *Say Say Oh Playmate*. They would sing the song, clapping each other's hands in intricate patterns, while going faster and faster until they couldn't go any more faster and would fall laughing into each other's arms. It was a wonderful way of connecting for them.

Sometimes Dan would come into the kitchen while Ann was making dinner and want to play. When Ann is focused on a task it's hard for her to take a break and be, playful. At one point, however, she realized that a playful interruption was a great way to connect with Dan and let him know he's worth it! So, when she was able, she would turn from her task and engage in their signature hand-clapping rhyme—a 30-second interruption that always ended in laughter, a hug, and feeling loved.

Play as Discovery

Play is more than a type of activity. It is an attitude that one brings to one's relationships and cicrumstances. It is a means of engaging one's relational partners—of discovering and connecting. When our immediate family gathers at the lake house that's been in my wife's extended family since 1891, an activity that builds some of the best memories and connection is washing the dishes together. Because dishwashing is done in a pan in the sink and we have minimal counter space, we need a team to wash, dry, put dishes away, and periodically launch biodegradable dishwater out the screen door into the forest. For whatever reason, this time often becomes one of singing, dancing, snapping drying towels at each other, and great laughter. If you are not washing dishes, you are missing out.

Essential here is that experiencing play means utilizing one's imagination and being focused, earnest (like a child at play), and fully present. If you are on your phone or distracted by some other task, you miss out on the "re-creation"[6] that is possible through discovering one another in new ways. Following, is how our *IPR* respondents described their playful experiences as creating space for discovery.

Discovery in the *IPR* responses showed up in a variety of playful ways. People talked about play creating an open and safe space that promotes self-disclosure,

> *You can mess around and they can mess around with you too and you can feel like you can really open up to that person.*

and they also told us that play shows up as imagination (new ideas) and the willingness to try new things in the relationship:

> *Play has demonstrated or created intimacy in a relationship of mine as far as being more creative and making things a little more interesting.*

When discovery involves risking and trying new things, some view play time as too risky for vulnerability (for example, when there is a competitive edge to the play), but a number of *IPR* participants actually referenced play as a time where one's defenses are lowered. Interestingly, this coincides with the conspicuous absence of fear in people's descriptions of play and intimacy. True play cannot take place in conjunction with fear. As we discussed previously, in order to create a safe relational space both partners need to be in agreement as to what constitutes play.[7] Lack of fear was often mentioned by our participants as freedom from being judged. The following quote is particularly interesting because it juxtaposes both fun and vulnerability with a lack of fear of judgment:

> *Play has created intimacy in my relationships by being able to allow myself to have fun and be vulnerable without being afraid of being judged and when I feel like i can let go is when I know the relationship is more intimate.*

---

6 Ashley Montagu, *Growing Young*, 2nd ed. (Westport, CT: Bergin & Garvey, 1989), 130–31.
7 As we saw in the previous example where a man and woman wrestled and ended up kissing, if the man's dominant physical positioning had been used for power, both play and intimacy would have ceased.

This quote underscores how a mindful approach to relationships (present, aware, no judgment) can create an intimate space where one can "let go" and *if something good can happen, it will.*

One of the good things that can happen during play is that you become free to be "you." A number of respondents mentioned that during play they were free to be themselves or, put another way, free to be their true self:

> *Being my true self has created intimacy because you are allowing someone to know you on a different level than others. You can take off the mask and be you. When you are silly and having fun you find a different type of love for someone.*

I was somewhat surprised at peoples' discussion of this aspect of play and intimacy. While it seems somewhat intuitive to think that intimacy is connected to sharing deeply with a relational partner, here we find that individuals also need to feel safe to express the silly and fun parts of themselves—without fear of judgment.

Play as Connection

Likely as you read about play and discovery you realized that the experience of vulnerability, risk, and finding and expressing one's true self happens within the context of connection. One of our respondents, besides getting points for using the word "concatenation," artfully described how novelty and discovery can bring people together:

> *Play has a way of truly bringing people together. Whether someone has shown you a new game to love, or a more efficient way to throw a ball, or even if you both thoroughly enjoy the same 'play' interests, our neurons of joy are set aflame and a concatenation of warm, happy feelings for that person, at that moment, overwhelm you. You then correlate this good feeling with that person's existence, and this creates a bond, or intimate feeling towards them.*

We see in this description how play brings a deep sense of bonding with and acceptance of the other person. And, this experience allows for a profound sense of presence and worth. Our respondents also emphasized that play creates a space for letting go and being present:

> *Play is a way to let go of inhibitions and be more present in the moment.*

For this individual, play leads to feeling safe (vulnerable) enough to drop inhibitions and be in the moment. Being present in this way sends a powerful connecting message—being with you, inhibitions dropped, is worth it. I'm willing to show up, when you are willing to show up—true self and all!

Let's look at one more way presence and worth are facilitated by play. Play is generally focused on an interaction, activity, or task for its own sake, not to achieve a task-oriented goal. This means that choosing to play with someone, to simply be with him or her without ulterior motive, can be powerfully affirming.

The following quote from a mom in our study describes intimacy, worth, and trust all developing as the result of simply taking time to play with her children:

> When my kids and I are involved in special play time where the child is leading the play activity, this shows that I believe my kids are worth spending time with and letting them take the initiative boosts their confidence. It is fun and builds trust which leads to intimacy.

Growing Close 3.4.2

Are you intrigued by some of the ways intimate experiences can be created through play? One of the often surprising aspects of play is that it can be a *safe place where if good things can happen, they will*. Basically, individuals' experience of play and intimacy reflects their ability to feel close and safe with others in ways that allow for vulnerability, connection, and the expression and value of one's true self. That's pretty good stuff. And it means that playful attitudes and experience can come from being silly or from feeling comfortable enough with someone to have a deep talk or share a meaningful activity. Is there a way you might bring a playful perspective to one of your relationships today?

Intimate Reflections

In the spirit of full disclosure, I should let you know that the only tattoo I have on my body is on my right ankle—it simply says *play*. One day, during the time when Ann and I were in counseling together, she said to me, "Play is really important to you, isn't it?"

"YES!" I calmly replied.

For some reason, play is one of the central ways I connect with others. If you and I can banter together, tease or joke with each other, or even wrestle with ideas we will likely be friends.

When my sons were little I playfully wrestled with them. As they got older, we added joking, playing games, and being silly to our play repertoire. This playfulness has continued to strengthen our connection and discovery of one another now that they're adults.

With my wife, Ann, she and I have learned to adopt a playful attitude toward romance and sex that is characterized by not taking ourselves too seriously, but seriously working together to discover and connect with one another. Adopting a playful relational frame has become a wonderful means of recreating this important aspect of our relationship.

In the next thread of this conversation, we turn our attention to what might seem the opposite of play—grief. Six years ago I lost my best friend, my mom, and my sister to cancer within months of each other. As grievous as this time was, it also created numerous opportunities for intimacy with those who were dying, as well as with those left behind. So, let's take a deeper look at how people experience grief as intimate space.

Thread 3.5

Intimacy Through Grief

E ight years ago I followed my friend, Dick, to a closet in his home where he retrieved seven spiral-bound notebooks. "These are my journals. When you read them you will understand why it's okay for me to die," he said, looking me in the eyes as he handed over to me his bound life. I stood silent. Stunned by Dick's vulnerability and trust of me. He had dealt with depression for a majority of his life and the cancer that was now racking his body was, in his own words, "God's grace."

Within 367 days of Dick's death, my mother and my sister would also die of cancer. It was an emotionally brutal year. One day, during this time, as I unlocked my office door I was greeted by a giant five-foot stuffed bear sitting at my desk. It didn't take me long to find out that it had found its way there with a little help from my friend and colleague, Vince Waldron. [1]

Grief. Intimacy.

When it comes to intimacy, grief may seem the antithesis of sex and play, but there are many ways that these paths to intimacy are similar. For instance, Vince's gift to help me "bear" my grief was certainly a

---

1 Vince and I have worked together for 25 years and co-authored and co-edited four books together, a number of which show up in the footnotes of this book.

healing, playful moment for me.[2] And, both sex and grief have aspects of feeling exposed, emotionally naked with others.

In this conversational thread we discover the relationship between grief and intimacy and acknowledge situations where grief can actually work against intimacy. We then zero in on how intimacy is experienced through grief, with a particular focus on how grief can open doors to emotional discovery and connection.

Grief and Intimacy (or not)

Most *IPR* responses to the prompt, *Please describe a time where grieving has demonstrated or created intimacy in one of your relationships*, focused on intimate moments with grieving friends, family members, romantic partners, or with those who were offering some type of emotional support. But some of those responses were intimate moments with the dying.[3]

Much like the moment where my dying friend, Dick, entrusted me with his journals, our respondents also reported this type of close encounter. One described simply spending time with her grandfather as part of growing close:

> *When I was 18, I moved to another state on my own. I had no car, and very little money. My grandfather started to get very sick, and was, ironically, life-flighted to a hospital across the street from my apartment. I spent every day with him, before and after work, and gradually watched him decline.*

Another told us of a promise made by an ex-boyfriend to a dying grandfather:

> *When my grandfather passed away about 4 years ago, it was a very hard time for me, and my ex boyfriend made a promise to my grandfather that he was going to take care of me, and he did just that. He made sure to make me laugh when I was going through such a hard time.*

Interestingly, one *IPR* participant experienced connection with someone who was dying and observed others turning away in fear of feeling deeply,

---

2 By the way, that bear has become a favorite wrestling buddy and resting place for my grandchildren!

3 For more on this topic, see a marvelous book by Maureen Keeley and Julie Yingling, Maureen P. Keeley and Julie M. Yingling, *Final Conversations: Helping the Living and the Dying Talk to Each Other* (Acton, MA: VanderWyk & Burnham, 2007).

I felt so close to her at a time when many turned away in fear of the depth of grief and pain from such a tragedy.

while another described intimacy with the dying and their own subsequent distance with the living:

To me, grieving has helped me feel very intimate with the deceased but in general has driven me away from other people who were grieving.

Still another participant described himself as one who simply doesn't show grief to others, because to do so would be to demonstrate weakness and ultimately hurt the relationship:

I don't grieve in front of others, no matter how much I want to. If I ever do, it lowers intimacy and I lose contact with them out of the feeling of showing weakness.

As the author of this last quote correctly discerns, grief leaves one vulnerable. It is for this reason that I included grief as part of the *IPR* study. Over the years I have become a big fan of grieving in my personal and professional life (in particular regarding my forgiveness research), because in many ways learning to grieve is essential to learning to live. When we are attentive, grief can teach us about vulnerability, emotional experience, making sense out of life, and how to grow close to others.

Growing Close 3.5.1

There is not a right or wrong way to grieve. Cultures round the world demonstrate a tremendous variety of approaches to grieving—some public, others private, some emotionally expressive, others reserved. How have you experienced and expressed grief? (Remember, grief can be more than a response to physical death. We can grieve the loss of a marriage, a job, a dream, or a beloved possession.)

Could grief be a means of going deeper in your personal relationships? Could letting "someone in" during times of grief be a means of developing connection with others?

Grief as Discovery

The vast majority of *IPR* respondents discussed grief and intimacy as occurring between those who shared a common loss or between the grieving and those who provided some type of comfort and support. People most often described grief situations as occurring within the context of the death of a family member or friend, including situations involving suicide and miscarriage, and a few described the loss of a beloved pet.[4]

Interestingly, expressions of grief (often including self-disclosure, crying, and hugging) occurred in close relationships with family and friends, but also with others less well known or not known at all. We experienced this at Ann's father's memorial service. Ann's father had been a well-known and beloved choral conductor at Arizona State University for twenty years. At his memorial, former students and colleagues who had been affected by his music and mentorship shared stories and tears with one another and with the family. These were intimate expressions, often between relative strangers who shared a common loss.[5]

All of the contexts for intimate experience that we have thus far discussed (talk, sex, play, grief), provide opportunity (like Ann's father's memorial service) to experience intimate moments that are not necessarily maintained and developed into intimate relationships. In this regard, it is important to remember that not all intimate moments are equal in terms of the levels of discovery and connection they create in the relationship as a whole.

Common experiences reported in the *IPR* study by those grieving were to feel vulnerable, exposed, and discovered by others, whether intentionally desired or not. As we just discussed, situations such as memorial services create intimate spaces where people may see us in our vulnerability. As the following quotes illustrate, these times can include strangers or those that feel like strangers:

Wanting to forget about everything and crying in front of complete strangers has demonstrated intimacy.

and,

---

4 In a previous conversation I confessed my love of dogs. A poignant intimacy memory, for me, is Ann, Daniel (my youngest son), and myself all lying on the living room floor with Allen, our beagle-lab mix, as he was put to sleep. Five years later, I still experience tears as I recall that beautifully intimate moment between the four of us.

5 These experiences were common in the sense of losing the same person, although certainly the relationships to the person lost were varied, even among family members.

My Aunt's funeral and seeing some of my family members after 30 years, and they felt like strangers to me. We shared tears, hugs, and stories for several hours and afterward five cousins re-established our relationships.

Of course, one can also experience vulnerability within the safe confines of a caring relationship, choosing to share with a trusted relational partner. In contrast to the two previous quotes, the following two accounts describe choosing to share pain with someone you trust:

When you let someone know you are grieving they learn you at your worst and most vulnerable. Trusting someone with your pain is very intimate. ...

and,

With gender stereotypes, its common for men not to cry or show any depressed emotion. However, my partner's close friend recently passed away. Since he trusts me, he was able to disclose how he felt emotionally.

The following quote (which would probably make director James Cameron extremely happy) describes vulnerability as being able to release your emotions in the presence of a loved one, feeling safe and accepted in their presence:

I was on a date when we watched the moving Titanic in the theater. The movie shook me in every possible way. I was beside myself crying, grieving and mourning the loss of all those beautiful people who lost their lives. I could barely make it to the parking lot where my car was parked. I could not stop the tears from pouring down my face. My date held me while I cried for at least an hour. I could not utter any discernible words, just tears. I felt an intimacy with him that night as he just allowed me to be and feel and express without any interruption or criticism.

As the previous quotes attest, whether by choice or simply feeling overwhelmed by emotion, the expression of grief and vulnerability with a loved one can be a sign of the quality of the relationship. One respondent described it like this:

Grieving has created intimacy because it is in this vulnerable state that you can tell how strong a relationship is.

This participant's perspective is an alternative to one offered previously by a respondent who chose to restrain from showing grief because it seemed like weakness. Of course, both perspectives are to some extent true. Grieving in the presence of others does make us vulnerable by revealing parts of who we are that may have been hidden up until this point. But it is this very vulnerability, when trust and safety are present, that strengthens and deepens the relationship.

Growing Close 3.5.2

Grief is different than our other intimacy contexts because there is more opportunity for emotions to overwhelm us and, as a result, for us to be "discovered," vulnerable without intentionally having decided to reveal ourselves. This vulnerability can be an important means of connection when you are with a safe and valued other. In my younger years I underestimated peoples' desire to "be there" for me, and I was too timid in "being there" for others. As I grew older and had more grief experiences I learned to let safe people into my intimate grieving spaces, and I better learned how to be a safe intimate space for others. Have you been open to discovering others through their grief? Have you allowed others to discover you when you were grieving.

Grief as Connection

Numerous *IPR* respondents told us they grew close to others during the grieving process. Closeness was in part driven by grief's ability to uncover parts of us previously concealed. One person described growing close by discovering parts of her friend that she didn't normally have opportunity to see:

When one of my best friend's grandpa passed away she was very upset by it. We were not that close at the time but being able to help her during her grieving process brought us closer. It made us more intimate because I got to see a side of her that I wouldn't normally see on an everyday basis.

The development of intimacy in this situation was also facilitated by the ability to help. We heard this frequently, both from those comforting and those being comforted. These intimate moments are characterized by asymmetrical reciprocal sharing—both parties are sharing (reciprocal), but they are sharing in different ways (asymmetrical—one is sharing by comforting, one is sharing by revealing grief). One of our male respondents told us:

> *I consoled my father after his dad's death. I had never seen my father cry up until that point in my life.*

And, one of our female respondents talked about being comforted by her boyfriend regarding her past sexual trauma:

> *As a sexual assault survivor, there are a lot of nights where I am really sad or disassociating and when my partner can help me to process my grief or just be supportive during, it can really help to foster intimacy.*

When words had a comforting effect on our grieving *IPR* participants it was often through a sense of mutual understanding. In the following quote, discovering similar experiences and feelings led to mutual trust of one another:

> *When my mom passed away, I talked to an individual that I worked with, but was not especially close with, and shared a feeling that I had. She too had the same feeling when her mom died and we talked and hugged and had a bond that brought us closer together. You never know what someone else goes through unless you share your own thoughts. I trusted her with my feelings, and she trusted me with hers.*

The essential part of these times, for many of our respondents, was simply being present with the other person. Presence was often associated with physical touch, mostly hugging and sitting close, but sex, for some. The following narrative provides a poignant example of the power of being present with someone, and using touch when words fail:

> *After my "big" sister's youngest son killed himself, I was uncertain what to do or say, until I saw her. In that moment, I just held her and didn't let go. In the days that passed, I was there as a calm presence and witness for her, letting her cry or sit in stunned silence. She always looked after me, and this time I got to take care of her.*

> ## Growing Close 3.5.3
>
> Has grief been uncomfortable for you as a griever or a caregiver? What if you decided it was okay simply to be present. Either present as someone cared for you or present as you cared for someone else. No words necessary. Two humans being—together. If you're really brave and it seems appropriate, you could take the risk of allowing or initiating caring touch—a hug or maybe an arm around the shoulders. Just enough to make your presence real.

Intimate Reflections

Grief is a powerful aspect of human experience. I've had to do a bit of grieving in my life and I find it to be incredibly healthy, even cleansing. One evening I was with a friend as we headed to California. We had been driving and talking all day long, he using that time as a safe place to process the fact that his marriage was failing. I was struck by the fact that the entire time he talked it was about logistics related to a potential divorce. What would happen if the relationship fell apart? What about his plans? His goals? That evening it occurred to me that I hadn't heard him express any grief over the loss of his wife, his dreams for the relationship, or all the emotional investment they had made as a couple.

I prodded, "Are you grieving the loss of all this?"

He sat quietly for a moment. "I don't know," he finally revealed. "I think I've been so wrapped up in either how to save the family business we've built, or plan for its demise, that I've never allowed myself to grieve."

A few weeks later we met at a local microbrewery and he reported to me, "I finally allowed myself to do some grieving. This is a huge loss for me."

I could hear sadness in his voice, but there were also signs of life. No longer numbing his pain, he was alive again. One of our respondents put it like this:

We grieved the loss of [our] relationship. We both knew it was going to end soon and we were falling out of love, but we still loved what we used to have.

That perspective sounds wonderfully healthy to me. Years after my wife's uncle died, the eyes of his widow would occasionally fill with tears during conversation—some small thing having reminded her of her beloved husband. This beautiful expression of her deep love always made me feel just a little closer to her.

Grief is a natural response when you lose something or someone you love. In the next thread of this conversation, we look at how intimacy finds its way into another context often associated with negative emotion. Let's take a look at how conflict can provide a somewhat counterintuitive means of partners connecting with and discovering one another.

Thread 3.6

Intimacy
Through Conflict

'm an only child. I grew up in an adult world of reason where all the resources (and homemade cookies) were mine. I never had to argue with siblings or fight to get my share. My parents divorced when I was seven years old. The only time I ever remember seeing them argue was a few weeks before my dad moved out. I was stunned. I didn't know that anything was wrong. But, one message was clear—*conflict leads to hurt, and hurt leads to people leaving.*

Later, this perspective became part of my dating strategy. If there was an argument I apologized before the anger and pain could fester and the other person end the relationship. In fact, this approach worked to maintain my relationship with my wife while we were dating, but ended up biting us in the relationship butt years later.[1] I knew, intellectually, that there could be good outcomes from conflict. In fact, after getting my doctorate I taught classes to that effect. Still, I ran from it. It made me uncomfortable and I presumed it made my relational partners uncomfortable, as well.

Some of you reading this introduction are resonating with it, while others are likely thinking, "I actually like conflict to a degree. It's stimulating and challenging." Just as we have seen with other intimate contexts,

---

1 More on this at thread's end.

people hold various perspectives on conflict and how it relates to intimacy. So, I begin this thread of conversation by overviewing a number of conflict perspectives that were evident in *IPR* participant stories, including general perspectives on the value of conflict, how to approach conflict, and potential conflict outcomes. Then, as in most *Conversation Three* threads, we will look at individuals' experiences of discovery and connection during conflictual situations. I finish this thread by discussing the role of comfort in intimacy. For most contexts, feeling comfortable with someone has been an important intimacy element. But, somewhat counterintuitively, with conflict we will find that being uncomfortable is essential to the process.

Conflict Overviews

No surprise that our *IPR* respondents viewed relationship conflict on a continuum from detrimental to normal to necessary. This variety of perspectives reflected participants' varied experiences with their partners. For some, conflict was relationally damaging, for others conflict seemed inconsequential (like siblings who just "brush it off"). Still others found conflict to be a means of embracing differences, showing respect, learning about one's partner, and strengthening the relationship. One participant sadly noted that conflict was the most effective way to get his father's attention:

> *I argue with my father a lot and I feel like it's needed because sometimes it's the only way I can get attention from him, even if I hate fighting with him.*

A few of our respondents also reflected on how conflict outside the relationship can serve to create intimacy within the relationship. The following quote identifies conflict with extended family members as something that draws together wife and husband:

> *Sometimes our family can frustrate my husband and our shared perspectives or opinions can help us feel closer in our relationship.*

Embedded in individuals' conflict stories were a variety of conflict styles, everything from being private and emotionally reserved to loud and emotionally expressive, and from emotions running high to emotions squelched for protection. Collaboration was noted fairly consistently as an approach to conflict that facilitates intimacy. The following quotes describe what it means to work through conflict together in order to strengthen the relationship:

Conflict has created intimacy because it furthers a relationship if the conflict makes us have to work together to further our understanding and knowledge.

and,

I wouldn't say conflict creates intimacy, but conflict resolution certainly did. Knowing that we might not always see eye to eye and working past things in order to create a stronger relationship.

Growing Close 3.6.1

What is your view of conflict? How has this view affected your personal relationships? What if you adopted the perspective that we might not always see "eye to eye" but working through things can create a stronger relationship? What if you began to view conflict as a means of discovery and connection?

Conflict as Discovery

The facilitation of intimacy through conflict was frequently described, by IPR participants, in terms of discovery. Discovery was often referenced as understanding the other's perspectives and emotions and learning from one another. The following quote came out of a situation where a young woman's boyfriend would take offense at her jealousy. Eventually, however, as they worked through the conflict it resulted in understanding:

I think every time me and my boyfriend have fights it helps him understand me more. Which creates closeness between us.

Another respondent described how parent and child conflict resulted in closeness through learning, not so much about their differences, but of their similarities:

My mom and I butted heads for the longest time, until I grew up and learned that we were very similar, which was often why we would end up fighting. These conflicts helped us grow closer.

In stark contrast to my own unhealthy avoidance of conflict (described at the beginning of this thread), consider the following description where the freedom to reveal emotion, absent the fear that it will damage the relationship, is a powerful means of maintaining intimacy:

It is the ability to be in conflict with my boyfriend but never afraid of that conflict ending the relationship because we both know the conflict is temporary and there are much more important things. I am willing to express my emotions without fear.

Significantly, these partners have created a relational space where it is safe to discover emotion. Similarly, the next quote comes from a woman who, in her late teens, wanted to move in with her boyfriend. She and her mom ended up in a fairly intense, prolonged conflict over this issue. However, a year later, when the cohabiting relationship fell apart, she found her mom to be a safe place for revealing her emotions and experience, and that her mom did not hold the past against her:

I went crying to my mom, and she was there for me in a heartbeat (just like she always was), but she never held anything against me for being brainwashed by this psychotic guy and acting the way I did. So moving forward, our relationship became a lot more intimate because I told her everything that had happened and I was really able to open up to her. She accepted me and was there for me the whole way through what I thought was the end of the world. Boy was I wrong. It was more like the best thing that could ever happen to me.

Evident in these last two scenarios is the important role that emotional safety and respect play in healthy conflict. These elements, as in the scenario above, can be facilitated when one party learns, or becomes aware, of the deep commitment of the other. The following quote emphasizes the connection between bonding and commitment—knowing "they will always love me":

Conflict with my parents. After every time I managed to mess up and argued with them over my actions, I always learned that no matter what I do they'll be there for me. Every time leads to an intimate bonding moment where I am constantly reminded that they will always love me.

Clearly, discovering the extent of someone's commitment to you and the relationship is deeply meaningful, but it also creates a safe space for partners to go deep with one another:

Conflict has created several issues in my relationships; however, it has revealed to me that in order to get to the depths of another person, you must know their likes and dislikes. From being in heated discussions and conflictual situations, I have learned the depths of my friends and because of that we have this unwavering bond.

Growing Close 3.6.2

As I've grown older, my conflict style has shifted from one that was primarily about defending my position, to one that involves more of a desire to hear from others. What if your approach to conflict shifted in the same way? Instead of digging in to protect your position, what if you created a safe place for discovery, allowing for understanding, sharing of emotion, and genuine learning from one another? What are some practical ways you can begin doing this today?

Conflict as Connection

As the previous quote indicates, discovery during conflict can lead to feeling more connected to others—*"because of that we have this unwavering bond."* Frequently, *IPR* participants described experiencing closeness as a result of conflict. As the following quotes make clear, closeness does not come easily, but is a result of sorting out differences,

My brother and I once had a fight where we literally did not speak for 2 weeks. It was really hard on our relationship obviously BUT it also brought us together because we were able to sort out our differences and

work towards a middle ground. It made us closer as siblings and I am thankful for a good outcome at least.

and learning through "bad or good" experiences:

Conflict that is resolved can be a lesson in a relationship. Lessons can become experience and experiencing things together as a couple, whether they are bad or good, can create a closeness/intimacy.

IPR respondents also told us they built connection through make-up sex or simply hugging after a conflict had been resolved. Affectionate touch appears to be a tangible way of reaffirming romantic couples' commitment to one another and, when distance has built up during conflict, rebuilding their physical and emotional connection. One respondent described this process with simplicity:

In order to grow in a relationship there must be conflict. If you get through that conflict there's the makeup sex.

Others noted that make-up sex provides a unique intimate experience in and of itself. The way a couple of respondents described this it almost makes you look forward to a little conflict:

Well when there's a conflict in your relationship once the two of you figure it out, there's nothing better than make-up sex.

and,

After an argument or verbally fighting, it seems as though making up with physical touch through intimate sex is as powerful experience of sex as is possible.

Presumably the heightened experience that accompanies make-up sex results from the high arousal and connection that have occurred during resolve of the conflict episode. Similarly, a couple of respondents saw the heightened state of fighting for an issue or for one's partner as a positive sign of commitment and intimacy. The following quote insightfully notes that conflict can reveal what is most important to us and, when engaged, can increase intimacy with our relational partner:

Conflict shows what is most important to you and what you are determined to fight for. Then your partner can work through it or let it go—which definitely shows how intimate you are with each other. The more willing you are to fight for something the better the chance to create intimacy.

The next quote also emphasizes the important idea of fighting in the relationship, but here the emphasis is on the choice to "fight for each other," even during disagreements:

It made us think. It made us dig deep and fight for each other even when we disagreed. In the end we both knew we wanted each other so it was worth the conflict and resolution.

To this point, as we discussed in *Conversation Two*, intimacy is much more complex than simplistic soulmate ideas. Both of the forgoing quotes suggest that intimacy emerges from or is enhanced by working through differences. This is especially the case when differences are treated with respect:

I believe periodic conflict or disagreement is essential for every healthy relationship. With diversity in opinions you tend to respect each other's perspective and develop a closeness in this process.

Growing Close 3.6.3

Can you begin approaching conflict in your personal relationships with a connection mindset? What if you saw working through differences as making you closer in your relationship? Making you stronger? More committed? Are there times where you can quit fighting over a particular issue and instead fight for one another? Fighting for one another involves being committed to your partner having a voice, even if her or his opinion is different than yours. One way to adopt this mindset is to view conflict as an outside threat to the relationship. From this perspective, instead of your partner being the enemy, you recognize the conflict itself as a potential enemy that threatens your relationship. You and your partner can then work together to resolve the conflict and protect your relationship, ensuring each of you has a voice in the process.

One last thought for romantic partners. What if instead of having "makeup sex" that is primarily feeding off of the high intensity from the conflict, you choose instead to reap the benefits of creative affection, tapping into the imaginative energy it takes to work together during healthy conflict?

Intimate Reflections

I don't think that it is an overstatement to say that being nice almost killed my marriage. Ann and I had confused being nice—avoiding conflict to keep the peace and make certain no one was made uncomfortable—with being loving and compassionate. At the beginning of this thread I mentioned that I avoided conflict by apologizing in order to keep the relationship intact. What I didn't share is that Ann avoided conflict by withdrawing. In this way, we created a perfect relationship storm that would eventually lead us to deep struggle and intense therapy.

One of the essential problems we had to deal with was our desire to keep each other comfortable. What we didn't appreciate was that, over time, we were stuffing our emotions and building emotional walls for self-protection. Years of operating this way prevented a deep intimacy from developing.

Thankfully, before it was too late, we learned that *the discomfort of conflict was the very thing that would help us create a space for the comfort of intimacy.*

As noted throughout this thread, respondents told us that it was the disruption experienced through conflict that allowed for new discovery and stronger connection. In this sense, good conflict creates an appropriately uncomfortable space where good things happen—a space where we can *safely* share information and express our emotions.

One way of creating this type of relational space is through forgiveness. Let's go to the next thread to see how forgiveness can create another appropriately uncomfortable intimate space where good things happen.

Thread 3.7

Intimacy Through Forgiveness

A few years ago I was part of a dissertation defense that focused on interpersonal forgiveness. At then end of the defense, one of the committee members asked the dissertation candidate, "Now that you've completed your research, has it changed anything about how you would choose to forgive?"

Rather surprisingly the candidate replied, "I would be more playful."

Playful? How could forgiveness possibly be playful? As she continued, I realized that what she meant by this was that she would try to hold the process and her expectations more lightly while staying open in the moment and creatively negotiating the intricate domain of forgiveness.

The idea of playful forgiveness has been intriguing to me, especially since I have devoted 20 years to the study of forgiveness[1] and have been interested in play and intimacy. Throughout my twenty years of studying forgiveness with colleague, Vince Waldron, we have learned that there are a variety of relational outcomes following forgiveness,

---

1 Douglas L. Kelley, Vincent R. Waldron, and Dayna N. Kloeber, *A Communicative Approach to Conflict, Forgiveness, and Reconciliation: Reimagining Our Relationships* (New York: Routledge, 2019); Vincent R. Waldron and Douglas L. Kelley, *Communicating Forgiveness* (Thousand Oaks, CA: SAGE, 2008).

including growing more intimate and strengthening the relationship, but we know less about how the forgiveness process can actually be experienced as intimacy with others.

So in this, our final intimacy context, we will look at *IPR* stories and anecdotes and explore how people experience intimacy through the forgiveness process. We'll begin with a quick overview of how people viewed forgiveness and the possibility of forgiveness creating a space for intimacy, and then look at elements of the forgiveness process can facilitate intimacy through discovery and connection.

Forgiveness Basics

As with all of our intimacy contexts, people gave us a variety of perspectives regarding forgiveness. Some saw forgiveness as essential to maintaining relationships, others had neither offered forgiveness nor ever received it. Of those individuals who reported a forgiveness experience, some had never experienced intimacy with forgiveness, but the majority had had some type of intimate experience.

As with previous forgiveness research that I have conducted, people reported a variety of relationship outcomes: relationship deterioration, relationship strengthening, return to normalcy, and redefining the relationship (for example, no longer dating, but still friends).[2] Forgiveness was generally associated with some type of relationship trauma, not just disagreement. And, some people identified specific actions that they couldn't forgive, such as infidelity. People also noted that forgiveness could be immediate or could take time as one attempts to make sense of what has happened and to manage emotions.

As you would guess, given that we asked for experiences where intimacy was associated with forgiveness, many *IPR* respondents described forgiveness as moving the relationship forward and creating a positive future. But some people's stories also highlighted potentially unhealthy perspectives regarding the role of intimacy in forgiveness. Note the following examples:

> *Forgiveness demonstrated intimacy in my relationship with my boyfriend because he could say something to me that is hurtful and no matter how*

---

2 Douglas L. Kelley, "The Communication of Forgiveness," *Communication Studies* 49, no. 3 (1998): 255–71; Douglas L. Kelley and Vincent R. Waldron, "An Investigation of Forgiveness-seeking Communication and Relational Outcomes," *Communication Quarterly* 53, no. 3 (2005): 339–58, doi:10.1080/01463370500101097.

upset I feel I will always forgive him and not even feel mad anymore because I love him.

and,

If I would ever get mad at my ex for doing something where I would have to forgive her, she would coerce me into having sex so I would forgive her faster.

We don't have the full story for these scenarios, but on the surface they both potentially involve manipulation, control, and possibly unhealthy emotional dependence. In contrast, other respondents highlighted elements of forgiveness that were more clearly part of building healthy relationships, such as choice,

Forgiving someone is not easy, especially if it is someone you love and or care about because their transgression is perceived to be much more impactful than someone you don't care about. Choosing to forgive someone creates intimacy for that reason—because I don't HAVE to forgive them.

not ruminating on the past, but moving toward the future,

Being able to let go of a negative to grow towards the positive is a way to strengthen a bond leading to a more intimate relationship.

and sacrificing in healthy ways that show your commitment to the relationship:

The ability to forgive amidst an ego issue has demonstrated intimacy for me because it shows his care and concern for my feelings and it shows his willingness to compromise his ego for the sake of the relationship. It is an admirable trait.

Another interesting forgiveness characteristic that may contribute to intimacy is the recognition of hurtful actions, yet, separation of those hurtful actions from the value of one's relational partner. One respondent, who presumably did something "wrong," described how receiving "undeserved mercy" helped him feel accepted as a person:

Forgiveness created intimacy because it allowed me to feel an undeserved mercy by my girlfriend which showed that she accepted me.

Another respondent amplified this perspective by recognizing the inherent value of being forgiven, but also insightfully noted the effect of recognizing and respecting their mutual sacrifice in the process:

When we forgive we achieve a higher position in any relationship and the other person feels the value of our absolution. With my partner, there have been moments when we have forgiven each other and thus grown close [intimate] by respecting our sacrifices.

Growing Close 3.7.1

What is your perspective on forgiveness? What has been your experience with forgiveness in your closest relationships? We are about to look at how forgiveness facilitates discovery and connection, but before we do, it will be helpful to think through what forgiveness is.

My colleagues and I have created a definition of *imaginative forgiveness*.[3] It's imaginative because it takes imagination to experience empathy for another human being and to imagine a new future. In the following definition, ask yourself about each bullet point, "Do I resonate with this? Do I struggle with this?"

Imaginative forgiveness is a relational process whereby,

- harmful conduct is acknowledged by one or both partners;

- both partners experience an emotional response and strive to make sense of their new relational situation;

---

3 Douglas L. Kelley, Vincent R. Waldron, and Dayna N. Kloeber, *A Communicative Approach to Conflict, Forgiveness, and Reconciliation: Reimagining Our Relationships* (New York: Routledge, 2019).

- the offending partner imagines the harmed partner's perspective and responds with remorse, sincerity, and full apology;

- the harmed partner imagines the offending partner's perspective, empathizes, and responds with mercy regarding the perceived transgression;

- partners experience a transformation from destructive to constructive cognitive, emotional, and/or behavioral responses;

- understandings of self, partner and relationship are reimagined and renegotiated;

- and possibly (re)enacted when safe conditions for reconciliation are created or restored.[4]

Forgiveness as Discovery

Because forgiveness always recognizes that something wrong or hurtful happened,[5] discovery (at least, of a transgression; at most, of characteristics of one's partner, one's relationship, or one's self) is inherent to forgiving or being forgiven. Hopefully this discovery includes openness and vulnerability within a safe relational space. As one *IPR* respondent put it:

> *For me, I've given forgiveness to my parents during times in our relationships that were very unhealthy. But to give and seek forgiveness is to acknowledge the undesirable behaviors we each have and to be seen in that light can open someone up in a way that typically isn't shown to others.*

Acknowledging "undesirable" behavior often occurs through apology. In fact, for *IPR* respondents apology was one of the most frequently discussed topics regarding discovery during the forgiveness process. In the stories that

---

4 This definition is somewhat prescriptive, intended to encourage others to use imagination to create healthy forgiveness processes in their relationships. For a more strictly academic definition, see Vincent R. Waldron and Douglas L. Kelley, *Communicating Forgiveness* (Thousand Oaks, CA: SAGE, 2008).

5 Douglas L. Kelley, Vincent R. Waldron, and Dayna N. Kloeber, *A Communicative Approach to Conflict, Forgiveness, and Reconciliation: Reimagining Our Relationships*, (New York: Routledge, 2019).

described some aspect of apology, sincerity stood out. The following quote recognizes the value of sincerity, especially since the storyteller's husband doesn't apologize very often. The uniqueness and vulnerability of the act contributed to feelings of closeness:

> *One time my husband did something stupid and said he was sorry, like genuinely sorry. He is not one to apologize often so I knew that he meant it. That made me feel closer to him and who he is as a person since he felt that he could be vulnerable and admit his mistakes to me.*

This type of sincere vulnerability is seen as a positive character trait, reaffirming the benefits of the relationship:

> *It takes strength and vulnerability to admit wrong doing, so forgiveness directly evokes intimacy. It's that grateful and admirable feeling towards someone that can take a step back and say I'm sorry.*

In a similar vein, another participant noted the character it takes to both seek and give forgiveness:

> *Asking forgiveness requires humility. Giving it requires generosity. Both of these qualities are important to create an atmosphere in which one feels comfortable being vulnerable.*

The last part of this quote is not to be missed—humility and generosity create an atmosphere where it's safe to be vulnerable. This is a mutual process that, as we have discussed so often throughout this book, helps to *create a space where if something good can happen, it will.*

Mutual discovery and apology were characteristic of IPR forgiveness discussions. The following scenario recognizes the value of going for a walk and talking together about forgiveness:[6]

> *Both my partner and I had made some pretty huge mistakes. In doing so we always made it a point to communicate even on the most difficult of topics. We went for a walk and spoke on the importance of forgiving. To truly forgive and how it would allow for both of us to grow. In this moment we*

---

6 Vincent R. Waldron and Douglas L. Kelley, "Forgiving Communication as a Response to Relational Transgressions," *Journal of Social and Personal Relationships* 22, no. 6 (2005): 723–42, https://doi.org/10.1177/0265407505056445.

expressed how deeply sorry we were and forgave one another which was very much needed.

Mutual discovery as part of forgiveness includes elements besides apology. For instance, the following quote succinctly identifies the importance of understanding, empathy, and learning about and from one another:

You understand each other's personality a bit more when you forgive someone, and you remember that it's important to be empathetic and learn from one another.

Another of our respondents told us a detailed story exemplifying these ideas. She began by describing her rather tumultuous history with her mom and how things were better when she eventually moved away. Somehow the physical distance allowed for different kinds of conversations to take place and eventually the development of more compassion and empathy. The culmination of this was a beautifully vulnerable time they spent together one evening. Take note of the empathy and understanding she exhibits while telling this story and the impact of having her hurt acknowledged:

She flew into town for my college graduation, and one evening, we were on the balcony laughing and drinking wine. She had made some joke about one thing or another, and tears came to her eyes. I asked her what the matter was, and she looked me in the eyes, so sincerely, and said, "I was a terrible mother. I was a terrible mother, and I am so sorry." She was not a terrible mother. She was a human who held on her back too heavy a burden than any person should carry. I think up until that point, there were absolutely some things I was subconsciously holding against her, but after that moment, I felt as if my hurt was acknowledged, and I was able to let it go. Today, our connection is stronger than I could ever have wished for.

This mother-daughter story represents many of the stories shared by our respondents. The honest expression of deep emotions was a means of discovery within the relationship. Mom's tear-filled eyes unearthed what she was thinking and feeling. This expression of remorse leading to feelings of closeness between mother and daughter.

Likewise, the following statement emphasizes how expressing feelings during an apology, can create space for discovery and connection between friends:

When I was open with another friend and apologizing for acting rude to them for not wanting the same thing as I did, during that openness I expressed my feelings. Expressing those feelings caused intimacy and closeness with one another.

Getting Close 3.7.1

In the stories we heard from *IPR* participants apology stood out as a means of discovery. What has been your experience with apology? Have you used or received perfunctory apologies, mostly intended to avoid having to deal with hurtful situations? Or have you experienced apologies that are sincere, intended to facilitate understanding and empathy, with an openness to learn more about the other?

Maybe there is something for which you have been waiting to apologize. Or, maybe you're thinking about an apology you made that was intended to "move on" quickly. How might you change your apologies so that they facilitate intimacy and understanding, instead of bypassing the problem?

Forgiveness as Connection

Forgiveness was often discussed by *IPR* respondents as related to connection. Certainly, this is in part due to asking for stories that demonstrated how forgiveness facilitated intimacy. But, also, common perceptions of forgiveness frequently include reconciling with one's estranged partners. It's important to recognize, though, that researchers typically make distinctions between forgiveness and reconciliation.[7] This is in part due to the risk involved if

---

7 Jason E. Kanz, "How Do People Conceptualize and Use Forgiveness? The Forgiveness Attitudes Questionnaire," *Counseling & Values* 44 (2000): 174–88, http://dx.doi.org/10.1002/j.2161-007X.2000.tb00170.x; Jill N. Kearns and Frank D. Fincham, "Victim and Perpetrator Accounts of Interpersonal Transgressions: Self-Serving or Relationship-Serving Biases?" *Personality and Social Psychology Bulletin* 31 (2005): 321–33, https://doi.org/10.1177/0146167204271594.

you think that forgiving a relational partner means staying in an unhealthy relationship. There is great freedom in knowing you can forgive, and make a separate choice as to whether it is wise to remain in the relationship. In this spirit, one of our respondents made clear distinctions between forgiveness and reconciliation:

> In all honesty, I forgive pretty freely, but that doesn't always mean I choose to maintain the relationship.

We want to be able to forgive and, yet, still choose whether to stay in the damaged relationship. Even more, we can use forgiveness to help create conditions for reconciliation when it is emotionally and physically safe to do so. In this regard, *IPR* participants frequently connected forgiveness with closeness in the relationship. We have seen this in a few previous quotes in this thread, but for good measure check out the following statement:

> There was an instance that I needed to be forgiven for an action I took years prior. When we finally worked it out there was an amazing feeling of closeness that I can't even begin to describe.

Interesting to me is that individuals also mentioned connection as occurring in response to certain forgiveness strategies. Stories described how minimizing (not making a big deal about it), gifts and restitution, and nonverbal displays could all be used to communicate closeness. The following description shows how minimizing and discussion were the beginning of a deeper forgiveness process:

> I got angry at something a friend did years ago and over time, I realized it wasn't a big deal and need to move beyond it. I eventually got in contact with the friend and forgave them and we ended up hanging out and sorting out our differences. I feel like forgiveness is what cleared up tension and made the friendship stronger, seems like we're closer friends than before so that's how it demonstrated intimacy.

This quote illustrates how opening the door through minimizing can lead to discussion ("sorting out our differences") and strengthening the overall relationship.

Another respondent reported what seemed a minor incident where restitution was needed. Interestingly, the restitution ended up having a big impact on reconnection—perhaps because the restitution was a surprise or revealed something about the offender's "true" character:

> One time, my fiancé forgave me for eating all her food in the fridge. After I bought her more food, she was happier than she was beforehand and we spent the rest of the evening together cuddling.

This short anecdote also demonstrates that forgiveness can be shown nonverbally, as in a return to positive emotion and nonverbal expression (cuddling). As we saw in the thread on conflict, makeup sex can also be a way of reconnecting and, even, communicating forgiveness:

> Sometimes sex can mean I forgive you in a relationship.

A final observation about demonstrating forgiveness nonverbally is that, at times, nonverbal expression provides emotional release. After the stress of the conflict, hugging it out can have physiological, as well as communicative, benefits:

> The embrace afterwards though was almost that of relief, and was a long embrace that had emotion and stress being relieved.

Growing Close 3.7.2

Is it surprising to you that forgiveness can create closeness? If so, try thinking of forgiveness as a complex process of discovery and, when conditions are right,[8] possibly connection. Remember that forgiveness often takes time.[9] That means we must be patient with our initial emotional response to being hurt. It's okay to be angry. And, it takes time to begin to heal emotionally and gain fresh perspective on what has happened. As you have read in some of our participant stories, when the time is right the forgiveness process can create shared experiences and reveal elements of character that may influence your thinking about potential reconciliation.

Intimate Reflections

A few days ago I was talking to a young man, married just one year, whose wife had told him, "You're not the person I thought I was marrying." In one sense, we all can appreciate what she means. However, there is another sense in which (re)discovering each other over the years is what marriage (or any long-term relational commitment) is all about. In this situation, the wife was learning to forgive her relatively new husband, not just for specific choices and acts, but for not being who she thought he was or, maybe better put, who she wanted him to be.

Author, Anne Lamott, puts it like this regarding her own mother, "I was annoyed in general because she is not at all whom I would have picked at the Neiman-Marcus Mommy Salon."[10]

Sometimes we simply have to forgive others for not being who we want them to be. I hope you hear the deep intimacy embedded in this. My forgiveness of you can say—*It's okay to be you*. That statement doesn't excuse "bad" or hurtful behavior. There is still work to be done. It simply says—*You are safe here. This is a space where good things can happen.*

---

8 Right conditions can include being emotionally and physically safe, and deciding that you are still interested in the relationship and that the relationship has the potential to be healthy.
9 As one of our respondents told us, forgiveness is your choice. I make it a practice of never telling someone they should forgive.
10 Anne Lamott, *Traveling Mercies: Some Thoughts on Faith*, (New York: Anchor Books, 1999), 209.

Thread 3.8

Intimacy as Relationship Art

A few years ago I created a website to keep people updated with what I do—mostly, what I'm writing and where I'm speaking. I played with a number of possible names for the site and settled with *RelationshipArt.com*. I chose this name because art represents a number of things for me.

First, art is imprecise in the way that relationships are imprecise—a blob of blue there, a streak of yellow over here can make all the difference.

Second, you don't always "get it." Sometimes you look at a piece of art and it just doesn't work for you. However, it might be amazing to the person standing next to you. We have friends who've been married almost 40 years. They are an anomaly to me. They never should have made it this long, but they've loved each other well during that time.

Third, art provides fresh perspective. Both art and relationships turn the world we thought we knew upside down.

Fourth, art helps manage the distinction between work and energy. Was writing this book a lot of work? At times. Mostly it took a lot of energy that I really loved.

Fifth, art is creative. If you haven't noticed, relationships are creative, too. The parts are always moving, requiring fairly constant adaptation. Sometimes you are jumpstarting the relationship with a creative edge. Other times you are figuring out how to respond to your fifteen-year-old daughter who wants to start dating.

Sixth, art is process. Unless you're painting by numbers, you don't just sit down, follow the rules, paint within the lines, and *Voila!* have the product you were looking for. Both art and relationships take shape ... over time.

Seventh, art is necessary, it is meaningful. It's not just "nice." Art and relationships constitute those things that touch our soul.

Finally, art is whimsy. It is playful, fanciful, imaginative, unpredictable. There is no one "right" way to do art ... or relationships. After all, they are both ... *ART!*

Making Your Relationship a Work of Art

With a few broad strokes I want to paint six themes that can help you and your partner create a relationship work of art. I recently gave a TEDx talk regarding these themes and their ability to help us discover one another, connect with one another, and be with one another.[1] They are largely derived from *IPR* stories, so a number of the following themes and quotes should have a familiar ring to them.

First, the idea of closeness. This has come up again and again throughout our discussions in this book and stood out in the responses from our *IPR* folks. Closeness can be experienced physically and verbally, but is more often a psychological sense of connection. We all are driven to be connected to something or someone. I love the following *IPR* quote regarding the impact of sharing the deepest parts of ourselves:

> *The relationship took on a more intimate nature as the level of self-disclosures increased. The more we shared who we are and how we exist in this world, the good and the bad, the more connected and intimate the relationship became.*

At the core of this quote is the second theme—being understood by others. This is a deep form of discovery. It's not just sharing with another human being and having him or her say, "Oh, I see. You really like peanut butter." It's about someone "getting" us. Truly understanding, "*Who we are and how we exist in this world.*"

---

1 Douglas L. Kelley, "Experiencing Intimate Spaces," filmed April 2019 at TEDxASU West, Glendale, AZ, video.

To be understood at this level[2] puts us in a deeply vulnerable place that is hopefully characterized by trust. The third theme, vulnerability and trust, highlights the deep connection that emerges when trust occurs in concert with vulnerability. Another favorite quote, that I introduced to you previously, beautifully portrays trust and vulnerability, along with the inevitable risk of being hurt:

Sex has created a sense of trust within my relationships. It shows that I am comfortable enough with you to let you see me at my most vulnerable. ... Sex is a soul tie so whenever I take that step with someone I am letting them in and giving them the chance to hurt me.

This woman is not describing a careless process of giving one's heart to anyone who asks for it. Rather, she trusts her partner. Her trust makes this a reasonable risk to take. And her courage to travel this road of relational discovery creates a profound sense of connection.

Trust and reasonable risk occur as we cultivate the fourth theme—presence. When we live out of a mindful posture, we live in such a way that we are present, aware of the other, without judgment. Why does it take so much courage to live this way? Perhaps because we have been hurt in the past and it feels so vulnerable to be truly known by another human being. That of course is why intimacy is ultimately experienced as presence and awareness without judgment. With. Known. Safe.

As I hope you can imagine, being present with another human being in this way creates a profound sense of worth, the fifth theme. As one mom told us, simply playing with her kids, having no other agenda other than being present with them, sends a powerful message—you are worth it. And, worth isn't simply a "feel good" idea. It is a necessary ingredient from which we build our relationships and our lives. Ann and I are the best partners to one another when we each believe that we are worth it! We have value. We can change and grow—together!

This brings us to the final theme—transformation into one's true self. This isn't just tweaking a few irritating behaviors. This is being secure enough, safe enough with another person, that you can take the risk of becoming.

Perhaps one of our *IPR* participants says it best:

[It's] that feeling of dropping your guard and becoming the absolute version of ... you.

---

2 Of course, as we discussed previously about art, this is process. This type of understanding takes time.

Closeness. Understanding. Vulnerability with trust. Presence and worth. All leading to the discovery and expression of your true self. It is only when we feel safe and connected that our true self emerges. And, for those who might worry that this is too much navel gazing, too much selfishness, consider this: when you feel safe to be *you*, you can quit spending so much time defending and protecting yourself. Instead, you are free to love others in ways that help to set them free as well.[3] Indeed, you are free to create your own ... *Relationship Art.*

---

3 Remember our discussion of full love (commitment, emotional bonding, and other centeredness) that creates a safe place for intimacy to exist.

BIBLIOGRAPHY

Ainsworth, Mary D. S., Mary C. Blehar, Everett Waters, and Sally Wall. *Patterns of Attachment: A Psychological Study of the Strange Situation*. Hillsdale, NJ: Lawrence Erlbaum, 1978.

Altman, Irwin, and Dalmas A. Taylor. *Social Penetration Theory: The Development of Interpersonal Relationships*. New York: Holt, Rinehart & Winston, 1973.

Altman, Irwin, Anne Vinsel, and Barbara B. Brown. "Dialectic Conceptions in Social Psychology: An Application to Social Penetration and Privacy Regulation." *Advances in Experimental Social Psychology* 14 (1981): 107–60. https://doi.org/10.1016/S0065-2601(08)60371-8.

Andersen, Peter A. "Researching Sex Differences within Sex Similarities: The Evolutionary Consequences of Reproductive Differences." In *Sex Differences and Similarities in Communication*, edited by Daniel J. Canary and Kathryn Dindia, 83–100. Mahwah, NJ: Lawrence Erlbaum, 1998.

Arendt, Hannah. *The Human Condition*. Chicago: University of Chicago Press, 1958.

Baxter, Leslie A. "Relational Dialectics Theory: Multivocal Dialogues of Family Communication." In *Engaging Theories in Family Communication: Multiple Perspectives*, edited by Dawn O. Braithwaite and Leslie A. Baxter, 130–45. Thousand Oaks, CA: SAGE, 2006.

Bem, Sandra L. "The Measurement of Psychological Androgyny." *Journal of Consulting and Clinical Psychology* 42, no. 2 (1974): 155–62.

Berkman, Lisa F. "The Role of Social Relations in Health Promotion." *Psychosomatic Medicine* 57, no. 3 (1995): 245–54.

Best, P., Manktelow, R., & Taylor, B. (2014). Online communication, social media and adolescent wellbeing: A systematic narrative review. Children and Youth Services Review, 41, 27–36. https://doi.org/10.1016/j.childyouth.2014.03.001

Bowlby, John A. *A Secure Base: Parent-Child Attachment and Healthy Human Development*. New York: Basic Books, 1988.

Bradbury, Thomas N., and Frank D. Fincham. "Attributions and Behavior in Marital Interaction." *Journal of Personality and Social Psychology* 63, no. 4 (1992): 613–28. http://dx.doi.org/10.1037/0022-3514.63.4.613.

Brown, Brené. "The Power of Vulnerability." Filmed June 2010 in Houston, TX. TEDxHouston video. https://www.ted.com/talks/brene_brown_on_vulnerability#t-12244.

Buber, Martin. *I and Thou*. Translated by Walter Kaufmann. New York: Charles Scribner's Sons, 1970.

Burgoon, Judee K. "Privacy and Communication." In *Communication Yearbook* 6, edited by Michael Burgoon, 206–49. Beverly Hills, CA: Routledge, 1982.

Burgoon, Judee K., Roxane Parrott, Beth A. Le Poire, Douglas L. Kelley, Joseph B. Walther, and Denise Perry. "Maintaining and Restoring Privacy Through Communication in Different Types of Relationships." *Journal of Social and Personal Relationships* 6, no. 2 (1989): 131–58. https://doi.org/10.1177/026540758900600201.

Buzzanell, Patrice M. "Resilience: Talking, Resisting, and Imagining New Normalcies into Being." *Journal of Communication* 60, no. 1 (March 2010): 1–14. https://doi.org/10.1111/j.1460-2466.2009.01469.x.

Buzzanell, Patrice M., and Lynn H. Turner. "Emotion Work Revealed by Job Loss Discourse: Backgrounding-Foregrounding of Feelings, Construction of Normalcy, and (Re)instituting of Traditional Masculinities." *Journal of Applied Communication Research* 31, no. 1 (2003): 27–57. https://doi.org/10.1080/00909880305375.

Carter, A. "Are Parents Having the Sex Talk with Their Kids?" HuffPost. November 1, 2017.

Ilona Croy. Isaac Sehlstedt, Helena Backlund Wasling, Rochelle Ackerley, Håkan Olausson. "Gentle Touch Perception: From Early Childhood to Adolescence," *Developmental Cognitive Neuroscience* 35, (2019): 81-86, https://doi:10.1016/j.dcn.2017.07.009

De La Lama, Luisa Batthyany, Luis De La Lama, and Ariana Wittgenstein. "The Soulmates Model: A Seven-Stage Model for Couple's Long-term Relationship Development and Flourishing." *The Family Journal* 20, no. 3 (2012): 283–91. https://doi.org/10.1177/1066480712449797.

Drescher, Amely, and Oliver C. Schultheiss. "Meta-Analytic Evidence for Higher Implicit Affiliation and Intimacy Scores in Women, Compared to Men." *Journal of Research in Personality* 64 (2016): 1–10. http://dx.doi.org/10.1016/j.jrp.2016.06.019.

Dwyer, Karen Kanga, and Marlina M. Davidson. "Is Public Speaking Really More Feared Than Death?" Communication *Research Reports* 29, no. 2 (2012): 99–107.

Emerson, Ralph Waldo. *Essays, First Series*. Auckland, New Zealand: The Floating Press, 2009.

Feeney, Judith A. "When Love Hurts: Understanding Hurtful Events in Couple Relationships." In *Feeling Hurt in Close Relationships*, edited by Anita L. Vangelisti, 313–35. New York: Cambridge University, 2009.

Feldman, Ruth, and Marian J. Bakermans-Kranenburg. "Oxytocin: A Parenting Hormone." *Current Opinion in Psychology* 15 (2017): 13–18. https://doi.org/10.1016/j.copsyc.2017.02.011.

Floyd, Kory. *Communicating Affection: Interpersonal Behavior and Social Context*. New York: Cambridge University Press, 2006.

———. "Human Affection Exchange: V. Attributes of the Highly Affectionate." *Communication Quarterly* 50, no. 2 (2002): 135–52. https://doi.org/10.1080/01463370209385653.

———. *The Loneliness Cure: Six Strategies for Finding Real Connections in Your Life*. Avon, MA: Adams Media, 2015.

———. "Relational and Health Correlates of Affection Deprivation." *Western Journal of Communication* 78, no. 4 (2014): 383–403. https://doi.org/10.1080/10570314.2014.927071.

Floyd, Kory, Justin P. Boren, Annegret F. Hannawa, Colin Hesse, Breanna McEwan, and Alice E. Veksler. "Kissing in Marital and Cohabiting Relationships: Effects on Blood Lipids, Stress, and Relationship Satisfaction." *Western Journal of Communication* 73, no. 2 (2009): 113–33. http://dx.doi.org/10.1080/10570310902856071.

Frederickson, Barbara L. *Love 2.0: How Our Supreme Emotion Affects Everything We Feel, Think, Do, and Become*. New York: Penguin Group, 2013.

Gilbert, Elizabeth. *Big Magic: Creative Living Beyond Fear*. New York: Riverhead Books, 2015.

Gottman, John M. *What Predicts Divorce? The Relationship Between Marital Processes and Marital Outcomes*. Hillsdale, NJ: Lawrence Erlbaum, 1994.

Grey's Anatomy. Season 1, episode 4, "No Man's Land." Directed by Adam Davidson and written by James D. Parriott. Aired April 17, 2005, on ABC.

Guerrero, Laura K. "Attachment Theory in Families: The Role of Communication." In *Engaging Theories in Family Communication: Multiple Perspectives*. 2nd ed., edited by Dawn O. Braithwaite, Elizabeth A. Suter, and Kory Floyd, 38–50. New York: Routledge, 2018.

———. "Emotion and Communication in Conflict Interaction." In *The SAGE Handbook of Conflict Communication*, edited by John G. Oetzel and Stella Ting-Toomey, 105–32. Thousand Oaks, CA: SAGE, 2013.

Guerrero, Laura K., and Megan Cole. "Moral Standards, Emotions, and Communication Associated with Relational Transgressions in Dating Relationships." In *Moral Talk across the Lifespan: Creating Good Relationships*, edited by Vince Waldron and Douglas Kelley, 155–81. New York: Peter Lang, 2015.

Guerrero, Laura K., Peter A. Andersen, and Walid A. Afifi. *Close Encounters: Communication in Relationships*. Thousand Oaks, CA: SAGE, 2016.

Guerrero, Laura K., Peter A. Andersen, and Melanie R. Trost. "Communication and Emotion: Basic Concepts and Approaches." In *Handbook of Communication and Emotion: Research, Theory, Application, and Contexts*, edited by Peter A. Andersen and Laura K. Guerrero, 3–27. San Diego, CA: Academic Press, 1996.

Hanh, Thich Nhat. *No Mud, No Lotus: The Art of Transforming Suffering*. Berkeley, CA: Parallax Press, 2014.

———. *Peace Is Every Step*. New York: Bantam Books, 1991.

Harlow, Harry F. "The Nature of Love." *American Psychologist* 13, no. 12 (1958): 673–85. http://dx.doi.org/10.1037/h0047884.

Hazen, Charlene, and Peter Shaver. "Conceptualizing Romantic Love as an Attachment Process." *Journal of Personality and Social Psychology* 52 (1987): 511–24.

Hemingway, Ernest. *A Farewell to Arms*. New York: Charles Scribner's Sons, 1929.

Hendrick, Susan S., and Clyde Hendrick. *Romantic Love*. Thousand Oaks, CA: SAGE, 1992.

Horowitz, Alexandra. *Inside of a Dog: What Dogs See, Smell, and Know*. New York: Scribner, 2009.

Iverson, Jana M. "Developing Language in a Developing Body: The Relationship Between Motor Development and Language Development." *Journal of Child Language* 37, no. 2 (2010): 229–61. https://doi.org/10.1017/S0305000909990432.

Jakubiak, Brittany, and Brooke C. Feeney. "Affectionate Touch to Promote Relational, Psychological, and Physical Well-Being in Adulthood: A Theoretical Model and Review of the Research." *Personality and Social Psychology Review* 21, no. 3 (2017): 228–52. https://doi.org/10.1177/1088868316650307.

Kanngiesser, Patricia, Bahar Köymen, and Michael Tomasello. "Young Children Mostly Keep, and Expect Others to Keep, Their Promises." *Journal of Experimental Child Psychology* 159 (2017): 140–58. http://dx.doi.org/10.1016/j.jecp.2017.02.004.

Kanz, Jason E. "How Do People Conceptualize and Use Forgiveness? The Forgiveness Attitudes Questionnaire." *Counseling & Values* 44, no. 3 (2000): 174–88. http://dx.doi.org/10.1002/j.2161-007X.2000.tb00170.x.

Kashdan, Todd B., and John E. Roberts. "Trait and State Curiosity in the Genesis of Intimacy: Differentiation From Related Constructs." *Journal of Social and Clinical Psychology* 23, no. 6 (2004): 792–816. https://doi.org/10.1521/jscp.23.6.792.54800.

Kashdan, Todd B., Patrick E. McKnight, Frank D. Fincham, and Paul Rose. "When Curiosity Breeds Intimacy: Taking Advantage of Intimacy Opportunities and Transforming Boring Conversations." *Journal of Personality* 79, no. 6 (2011): 1067–99. https://doi.org/10.1111/j.1467-6494.2010.00697.x.

Kearns, Jill N., and Frank D. Fincham. "Victim and Perpetrator Accounts of Interpersonal Transgressions: Self-Serving or Relationship-Serving Biases?" *Personality and Social Psychology Bulletin* 31 (2005): 321–33. https://doi.org/10.1177/0146167204271594.

Keeley, Maureen P., and Julie M. Yingling. *Final Conversations: Helping the Living and the Dying Talk to Each Other*. Acton, MA: VanderWyk & Burnham, 2007.

Kelley, Douglas L. "The Communication of Forgiveness," *Communication Studies* 49, no. 3 (1998): 255–71.

——. "Doing Meaningful Research: From No Duh to Aha! (A Personal Record)." *Journal of Family Communication* 8, no. 1 (2008): 1–18.

——. "Experiencing Intimate Spaces." Filmed April 2019 in Glendale, AZ. TEDxASUWest, video. https://www.ted.com/talks/douglas_kelley_experiencing_intimate_space_six_ways_people_experience_intimacy

——. *Just Relationships: Living Out Social Justice as Mentor, Family, Friend, and Lover*. New York: Routledge, 2017.

——. "Just Relationships: A Third Way Ethic." *The Atlantic Journal of Communication* (2019). DOI: 10.1080/15456870.2020.1684290

——. *Marital Communication*. Cambridge, England: Polity Press, 2012.

——. "Privacy in Marital Relationships." *Southern Speech Communication Journal* 53, no. 4 (1988): 441–56. https://doi.org/10.1080/10417948809372741.

——. "Understanding Relational Expectations and Perceptions of Relational Satisfaction in Marital Relationships." PhD diss., University of Arizona, 1988.

Kelley, Douglas L., and Vincent R. Waldron. "An Investigation of Forgiveness-seeking Communication and Relational Outcomes." *Communication Quarterly* 53, no. 3 (2005): 339–58. https://doi.org/10.1080/01463370500101097.

Kelley, Douglas L., Vincent R. Waldron, and Dayna N. Kloeber. *A Communicative Approach to Conflict, Forgiveness, and Reconciliation: Reimagining Our Relationships*. New York: Routledge, 2019.

Kim, J., & Lee, J. E. R. (2011). The Facebook paths to happiness: Effects of the number of Facebook friends and self-presentation on subjective well-being. *Cyberpsychology, Behavior, and Social Networking*, 14, 359–364.

Knapp, Mark L. *Interpersonal Communication and Human Relationships*. Boston: Allyn & Bacon, 1984.

Knapp, Mark L., Donald G. Ellis, and Barbara A. Williams. "Perceptions of Communication Behavior Associated with Relationship Terms." *Communications Monographs* 47, no. 4 (1980): 262–78. https://doi.org/10.1080/03637758009376036.

Knapp, Mark L., Anita L. Vangelisti, and John P. Caughlin. *Interpersonal Communication and Human Relationships*, 7th ed. Boston: Allyn & Bacon/Pearson, 2013.

The Knot. "Traditional Wedding Vows From Various Religions." Theknot.com. June 07, 2019. Accessed June 24, 2019. https://www.theknot.com/content/traditional-wedding-vows-from-various-religions.

Koenig Kellas, Jody. "Communicated Narrative Sense-Making Theory: Linking Storytelling and Well-being." In *Engaging Theories in Family Communication: Multiple Perspectives*. Edited by Dawn O. Braithwaite, Elizabeth A. Suter, and Kory Floyd, 62–74. New York: Routledge, 2018.

Kübler-Ross, Elizabeth, and David Kessler. *On Grief and Grieving: Finding the Meaning of Grief Through the Five Stages of Loss*. New York: Simon & Schuster, 2005.

Lamott, Anne. *Traveling Mercies: Some Thoughts on Faith*. New York: Anchor Books, 1999.

Lampis, Jessica, Stefania Cataudella, Alessandra Busonera, and Elizabeth A. Skowron. "The Role of Differentiation of Self and Dyadic Adjustment in Predicting Codependency." *Contemporary Family Therapy* 39, no. 1 (2017): 62–72. https://doi.org/10.1007/s10591-017-9403-4.

Manusov, Valerie. "Mindfulness as Morality: Awareness, Nonjudgment, and Nonreactivity in Couples' Communication." In *Moral Talk across the Lifespan: Creating Good Relationships*, edited by Vincent Waldron and Douglas Kelley, 183–201. New York: Peter Lang, 2015.

Manusov, Valerie. "Reacting to Changes in Nonverbal Behaviors Relational Satisfaction and Adaptation Patterns in Romantic Dyads." *Human Communication Research* 21, no. 4 (1995): 456–477. https://doi.org/10.1111/j.1468-2958.1995.tb00354.x.

Manusov, Valerie and Brian H. Spitzberg. "Attributes of Attribution Theory: Finding Good Cause in the Search for Theory." In *Engaging Theories in Interpersonal Communication: Multiple Perspectives*, edited by Dawn O. Braithwaite and Leslie A. Baxter, 37–49. Thousand Oaks, CA: SAGE, 2008.

Mineo, Liz. "Good Genes Are Nice, But Joy is Better." *The Harvard Gazette*. Accessed June 22, 2019. https://news.harvard.edu/gazette/story/2017/04/over-nearly-80-years-harvard-study-has-been-showing-how-to-live-a-healthy-and-happy-life/.

Minuchin, Salvador. *Families and Family Therapy*. Cambridge: Harvard University Press, 1974.

Mirivel, Julien C. "Communication Excellence: Embodying Virtues in Interpersonal Communication." In *Positive Communication in Interpersonal Relationships*, edited by Thomas J. Socha and Margaret J. Pitts. New York: Peter Lang, 2012.

Montagu, Ashley. *Growing Young*. 2nd ed. Westport, CT: Bergin & Garvey, 1989.

MultiVu. "Cigna U.S. Loneliness Index." Accessed June 26, 2019. https://www.multivu.com/players/English/8294451-cigna-us-loneliness-survey/docs/IndexReport_1524069371598-173525450.pdf.

MultiVu. "New Cigna Study Reveals Loneliness at Epidemic Levels in America." Accessed June 26, 2019. https://www.multivu.com/players/English/8294451-cigna-us-loneliness-survey/.

Murray, Sandra L., Jaye L. Derrick, Sadie Leder, and John G. Holmes. "Balancing Connectedness and Self-Protection Goals in Close Relationships: A Levels-of-Processing Perspective on Risk Regulation." *Journal of Personality and Social Psychology* 94, no. 3 (2008): 429–59. https://doi.org/10.1037/0022-3514.94.3.429.

Ni, Hua-Ching, and Mao Shing Ni with Joseph Miller. *Tai Chi for a Healthy Body, Mind and Spirit*. Los Angeles: Tao of Wellness Press, 2011.

Norfleet, Agnes W. "Genesis Commentary." In *The Renovaré Spiritual Formation Study Bible*, edited by Richard J. Foster. San Francisco: HarperCollins, 1989.

Obert, Julia C. "What We Talk About When We Talk About Intimacy." *Emotion, Space, and Society* 21 (2016): 25–32.

Oxford English Dictionary (Oxford, UK: Oxford University Press, 2019).

Palmer, Parker J. *The Promise of Paradox: A Celebration of Contradictions in the Christian Life*. Hoboken, NJ: John Wiley & Sons, 2010.

Perel, Esther, and Peter Sagal. "Not My Job: We Quiz Couples Therapist Esther Perel on The Monastic Life," June 10, 2017. In *Wait Wait … Don't Tell Me!* Produced by Mike Danforth. Podcast. https://www.npr.org/2017/06/10/532171202/not-my-job-we-quiz-couples-therapist-esther-perel-on-the-monastic-life.

Petronio, Sandra. "Communication Boundary Management: A Theoretical Model of Managing Disclosure of Private Information Between Marital Couples." *Communication Theory* 1, no. 4 (1991): 311–35. https://doi.org/10.1111/j.1468-2885.1991.tb00023.x.

———. *Boundaries of Privacy: Dialectics of Disclosure*. Albany, NY: State University of New York Press, 2002.

Prager, Karen J. *The Psychology of Intimacy*. New York: Guilford Press, 1995.

Reznik, Rachel M., Michael E. Roloff, and Courtney W. Miller. "There is Nothing as Calming as a Good Theory: How a Soulmate Theory Helps Individuals Experience Less Demand/Withdraw and Stress." In *Communicating Interpersonal Conflict in Close Relationships*, edited by Jennifer A. Samp, 37–46. New York: Routledge, 2016.

Roddenberry, Gene. *Star Trek: The Original Series*. Hollywood, CA: NBC, 1969.

Rusbult, Caryl E., Peggy A. Hannon, Shevaun L. Stocker, and Eli J. Finkel. "Forgiveness and Relational Repair." In *Handbook of Forgiveness*, edited by Everett L. Worthington, Jr., 185–205. New York: Routledge, 2005.

Sanford, Keith. "Hard and Soft Emotion During Conflict: Investigating Married Couples and Other Relationships." *Personal Relationships* 14, no. 1 (April 2007): 65–90. https://doi.org/10.1111/j.1475-6811.2006.00142.x.

Satir, Virginia. *Conjoint Family Therapy: A Guide to Theory and Technique*. Palo Alto: Science and Behavior Books, 1967.

Shore, Rima. *Rethinking the Brain: New Insights into Early Development*. New York: Families and Work Institute, 1997.

Spitzberg, Brian H., and William R. Cupach. *Handbook of Interpersonal Communication Competence*. New York: Springer-Verlag, 1988.

Stanley, Scott M., Sarah W. Whitton, Sabina Low Sadberry, Mari L. Clements, and Howard J. Markman. "Sacrifice as a Predictor of Marital Outcomes." *Family Process* 45, no. 3 (2006): 289–303. https://doi.org/10.1111/j.1545-5300.2006.00171.x.

Sternberg, Robert J. *The Triangle of Love: Intimacy, Passion, Commitment*. New York: Basic, 1988.

———. "A Triangular Theory of Love." *Psychological Review* 93 (1986): 119–35.

———. "Triangular Theory of Love." In *Encyclopedia of Social Psychology*, edited by Roy F. Baumeister and Kathleen D. Vohs, 998. Thousand Oaks, CA: SAGE, 2007.

———. "Triangulating Love." In *The Psychology of Love*, edited by Robert J. Sternberg and Michael L. Barnes, 119–38. New Haven, CT: Yale University Press, 1988.

Stewart, John. *Bridges Not Walls: A Book about Interpersonal Communication*. 11th ed. New York: McGraw-Hill, 2012.

Suter, Elizabeth A., and Leah M. Seurer. "Relational Dialectics Theory: Realizing the Dialogic Potential of Family Communication." In *Engaging Theories in Family Communication: Multiple Perspectives*, edited by Dawn O. Braithwaite, Elizabeth A. Suter, and Kory Floyd, 62–74. New York: Routledge, 2018.

Taylor, Paul, Cary Funk, and Peyton Craighill. "Gauging Family Intimacy: Dogs Edge Cats (Dads Trail Both)." Retrieved from Pew Research Center: A Social Trends Report. http://assets.pewresearch.org/wp-content/uploads/sites/3/2010/10/Pets.pdf.

Tomlinson, Edward C. "The Impact of Apologies and Promises on Post-Violation Trust: The Mediating Role of Interactional Justice." *The International Journal of Conflict Management* 23, no. 3 (2012): 224–47. https://doi.org/10.1108/10444061211248930.

Tracy, Sarah J. *Qualitative Research Methods: Collecting Evidence, Crafting Analysis, Communicating Impact*. West Sussex, UK: John Wiley & Sons, 2013.

Trees, April R. "Attachment Theory: The Reciprocal Relationship Between Communication and Attachment Patterns." In *Engaging Theories in Family Communication: Multiple Perspectives*, edited by Dawn O. Braithwaite and Leslie A. Baxter, 165–80. Thousand Oaks, CA: SAGE, 2006.

Tutu, Desmond. *No Future Without Forgiveness*. New York, NY: Doubleday, 1999.

Vanauken, Sheldon. *A Severe Mercy*. New York: Bantam, 1977.

Waldron, Vincent R., and Douglas L. Kelley. *Communicating Forgiveness*. Thousand Oaks, CA: SAGE, 2008.

———. "Forgiving Communication as a Response to Relational Transgressions." *Journal of Social and Personal Relationships* 22, no. 6 (2005): 723–42. https://doi.org/10.1177/0265407505056445.

Waldron, Vincent R., Dayna Kloeber, Carmen Goman, Nicole Piemonte, and Joshua Danaher. "How Parents Communicate Right and Wrong: A Study of Memorable Moral Messages Recalled by Emerging Adults." *Journal of Family Communication* 14, no. 4 (2014): 374–97. https://doi.org/10.1080/15267431.2014.946032.

Watzlawick, Paul, Janet B. Bavelas, and Don D. Jackson. *Pragmatics of Human Communication: A Study of Interactional Patterns, Pathologies and Paradoxes*. New York: W.W. Norton & Company, 2011.

Whitton, Sarah W., Scott M. Stanley, and Howard J. Markman. "If I Help My Partner, Will It Hurt Me? Perceptions of Sacrifice in Romantic Relationships." *Journal of Social and Clinical Psychology* 26, no. 1 (2007): 64–91. https://doi.org/10.1521/jscp.2007.26.1.64.

Whyte, David, and Krista Tippett. "The Conversational Nature of Reality." In *On Being with Krista Tippett*. April 7, 2016. Podcast. https://onbeing.org/programs/david-whyte-the-conversational-nature-of-reality-dec2018/.

Williams, Mason. *You Done Stomped on My Heart*. New York: RCA Records, 1969. Performed by John Denver.

Worthington, Everett L. Jr., *Forgiveness and Reconciliation: Theory and Application*. New York: Routledge, 2006.

Worthington, Everett L., Jr., and Dewitt T. Drinkard. "Promoting Reconciliation Through Psychoeducational and Therapeutic Interventions." *Journal of Marital and Family Therapy* 26, no. 1 (2000): 93–101. https://doi.org/10.1111/j.1752-0606.2000.tb00279.x.

INDEX

CPSIA information can be obtained
at www.ICGtesting.com
Printed in the USA
FSHW020856191220
76987FS